D0368113

THE TRUTH ABOUT SUCKING UP

How Authentic Self-Promotion Benefits You and Your Organization

Center for Creative Leadership

www.ccl.org

The Center for Creative Leadership is an international, nonprofit educational institution founded in 1970 to advance the understanding, practice, and development of leadership for the benefit of society worldwide. As a part of this mission, it publishes books and reports that aim to contribute to a general process of inquiry and understanding in which ideas related to leadership are raised, exchanged, and evaluated. The ideas presented in its publications are those of the author or authors.

The Center thanks you for supporting its work through the purchase of this volume. If you have comments, suggestions, or questions about any CCL Press publications, please contact the Director of Publications at the address given below.

Center for Creative Leadership
Post Office Box 26300
Greensboro, North Carolina 27438-6300
Telephone 336 288 7210
www.ccl.org

Gina Hernez-Broome
Cindy McLaughlin
Stephanie Trovas

THE TRUTH ABOUT SUCKING UP

How Authentic Self-Promotion Benefits You and Your Organization

CENTER FOR CREATIVE LEADERSHIP
Greensboro, North Carolina

CCL Stock Number 191
©2009 Center for Creative Leadership

Published by CCL Press
Sylvester Taylor, Director of Assessment, Tools, and Publications
Peter Scisco, Editor, CCL Press
Karen Lewis, Associate Editor

Design and layout by Joanne Ferguson, Clinton Press

Library of Congress Cataloging-in-Publication Data

Hernez-Broome, Gina.
    The truth about sucking up : how authentic self-promotion benefits you and your organization / Gina Hernez-Broome, Cindy McLaughlin, Stephanie Trovas.
        p. cm.
    ISBN 978-1-60491-067-4
1. Promotions. 2. Organizational behavior. I. McLaughlin, Cindy.
II. Trovas, Stephanie. III. Title.

    HF5549.5P7H47 2009
    650.1'3--dc22

                                                                2009012510

CONTENTS

ACKNOWLEDGMENTS

The idea to write this book came after many lively discussions about how certain people in the workplace are consistently in the limelight while others work diligently yet linger in obscurity. Through our work with leaders and our research efforts, we have coached, consoled, and advised hundreds of people who are disappointed to learn that others don't share their own views of their skills and contributions. We discovered that this difference in perception often has more to do with the visibility of people and their work than with how effectively they employ their strengths. It's unfair, it's not right, and it's not productive— but it is the truth. We heard stories, witnessed behaviors, and experienced this phenomenon ourselves. Our book sheds light on something that we all know exists but we often don't want to confront. Authentic self-promotion is a necessary part of being successful in the workplace. It's helpful to you, your team, and your organization. Sucking up is not. We have done our best to clarify the differences between sucking up and authentic self-promotion, to provide helpful insights, and to reframe the topic in a beneficial, practical manner.

We gratefully acknowledge all the people in our professional and personal lives who shared their strong beliefs and colorful examples with us. They made writing this book fun. Most notably, we thank our husbands—Eric, Jim, and Jeff—for sharing their beliefs and providing great examples of people who don't self-promote. We graciously offer our thanks to Pete Scisco. Without his willingness to take a risk, these words would never have emerged. We offer special gratitude to Rebecca Garau, who made our words sensible. We have some tremendously supportive colleagues and family members who continue to offer suggestions and examples. We are especially grateful to Sue Lundberg,

Gina Schaarschmidt, and Bruce Byington. Finally, we wish to acknowledge Karen Lewis, Rich Marcy, Rola Ruohong Wei, and Vanessa Benozzi for their careful review of early drafts of our book.

INTRODUCTION

Self-promotion gets a bad rap. Many people in organizations revile its practice, and they belittle the people who adopt its tactics with derogatory labels like *brownnosers* and *suck-ups*. Yet, time after time, organizations reward self-promoters. Rewards and opportunities are routinely bestowed on the most vocal or most visible even if they aren't the most qualified. The peers and direct reports of self-promoters may dismiss them as braggarts, attention hogs, and manipulators, but the people who shine a light on themselves (or somewhere else, if you listen to their detractors) are inevitably first in line for promotions, funding, and plum assignments.

How can this be? How can authentic performance lose out to grandstanding? Why does this disconnect occur? Employees at all levels of organizations wonder why leaders overlook and even reward what they themselves see as clearly bad behavior. Why aren't the suck-ups seen for what they really are? Why aren't they held accountable for their outlandish promises or for claiming credit for group accomplishments? If organizations don't routinely notice good work, how do they distinguish between effective self-promotion and sucking up?

These are frank questions—too often undiscussable, yet critically important. Beyond the bruised egos or the free-floating sense of unfairness that employees may feel lies a larger organizational problem: when the wrong people get noticed and rewarded, organizations suffer. Projects fail, goals are not met, and employee morale and motivation disintegrate. Cynicism festers, undermining sincere efforts at employee development, talent management, and succession planning.

What can you do to change these drastic outcomes? To start, you can learn to make self-promotion part of your everyday work life. You can learn to become a skilled self-promoter while maintaining your ethical boundaries and your authenticity. You can learn to appreciate this truth about sucking up: your negative response to self-aggrandizing behavior can mask real benefits of appropriate self-promotion. You may not want to "play that game," but don't refuse a seat at the table. It is possible to identify the worst suck-ups in your organization and to develop effective promotional strategies that you can use to counter their moves.

Self-promotion does have potential pitfalls, but doing nothing has certain perils. If you get a handle on the dynamics of self-promotion and the effects it can have on your individual career, you can learn how to promote yourself without selling your soul or becoming a suck-up. There is a line between seeking earned visibility and demanding unwarranted attention, and this book can help you find that line in yourself, in your group, and in your organization.

But that's not the end of it. In this book we also extend those lessons to highlight the relationship between self-promotion and your organization's success. We know that most managers—whether group leaders, project managers, mid-level managers, or top executives—play a dual role when it comes to the dynamics of self-promotion. Not only do you have the responsibility to promote yourself, your employees, and the work of your group, but you also receive plenty of promotional appeals from others. To remain effective—to avoid getting taken in by the suck-ups around you and to enhance your organization's ability to develop talent to its full potential—you must discern and judge the messages and the messengers that come your way.

Why Self-Promotion Matters

Many talented, effective individuals avoid promoting themselves and their work. As managers or group leaders, they resist

Top Ten Reasons Self-Promotion Has a Bad Reputation

How often have you witnessed these distasteful outcomes result from unscrupulous self-promoting behavior?

1. Over-the-top self-promotion is at the expense of others.
2. The best person for the job is overlooked.
3. It's all about *me* instead of *us*.
4. You schmooze or you lose.
5. Spin trumps truth.
6. Charisma triumphs over substance.
7. Bragging and boasting are rewarded over performance.
8. Visibility hides incompetence.
9. Steady performers are overlooked or penalized.
10. Arrogance is confused with expertise.

talking up the group and its accomplishments. Unfortunately, by not promoting their work, these talented individual contributors, up-and-coming leaders, and even experienced managers miss out on rewarding opportunities and new experiences, positive recognition and reward, and increased confidence, credibility, and influence.

Plus, the organization misses out. The wrong person may be put in a job, frustrating both the employee and those with whom he works. In some cases, the skill set isn't a match or the level of skill isn't where it needs to be. Other times, potential talent is underutilized. People have abilities and interests that go beyond the scope of their job descriptions, but they are not recognized and put to use. The organization also loses out when information is held closely. Information and insight about competition or customers, effective processes or new solutions, and opportunities or challenges, for instance, all have value outside a single group or department.

In highly competitive industries and during difficult economic times, organizations cannot afford multiple missteps caused by misjudging and misusing their talent. Yet studies show that this is happening all the time.

- In a CCL study using 360-degree performance data, results showed that more than one-third of all managers and leaders are undervalued by their superiors and peers. Many of these people are top performers in their organizations, but because they do not self-promote, their talents are often unseen and even lost to their organizations.

- A study conducted by Career Systems International revealed that 77 percent of employees believe they have more abilities than they are currently using.

- According to a worldwide employee engagement study conducted by BlessingWhite, Inc., nearly 45 percent of global employees feel that their managers do not recognize their good work or encourage them to use their talents. What's more, 40 percent of employees surveyed indicated that they are currently planning their escape as a result. That translates to high cost and lost productivity for organizations that have not yet mastered the art of creating an effective environment where talent is recognized, rewarded, and fostered. During times of economic turmoil, recognizing talent becomes even more critical. Companies faced with staff reductions and operating on lean budgets simply cannot afford to lose their best performers.

At the same time, senior executives cite a shortage of talent as one of the top factors contributing to increasingly complex business challenges.

While the lack of skillful self-promotion isn't the only reason for this organizational talent gap, it is a contributing factor. A company may not need to look any further than the talent that is already in the organization but often not recognized.

In his influential book *Good to Great*, Jim Collins writes about the importance of talent. He describes the key to organizational success as "getting the right people on the bus." We agree with Collins, but think he underestimates the challenge of knowing and identifying your talent pool. The only way to get the right people on the bus is to know who is there and who is missing. This allows you to decide who should be on the bus and whether someone needs to get off at the next stop! Another risk is that, in your haste to get to the next stop, you may leave a talented person standing at the bus stop or running frantically to catch the bus.

Of course, it's hard to know what talent exists in your organization. Who *are* the right people? Organizations and managers can make the most of existing talent only if individual skills, abilities, and accomplishments are known. And if some people are reluctant to speak up about their abilities and others put a positive spin on everything they do, it's all too easy to get the wrong people in the wrong seats on the bus.

What's Your Responsibility?

Self-promotion is by definition promoting yourself; in that regard it *is* self-serving. Self-promotion is self-serving in the same way that networking or skill building is self-serving: it is a way for you to steer your career. But you also have to take responsibility to ensure that your skills, interests, and abilities are put to good use in the organization. This, too, requires self-promotion. These are your responsibilities:

- Understand yourself. Get clear on your strengths and why they matter. If you try to self-promote and are off the mark, then you come across as either pathetic or having delusions of grandeur.

- Back up your claims with real accomplishments, skills, experience, or knowledge that deserves recognition and acknowledgment.

- Practice and improve your ability to talk about yourself. Be assertive, communicative, but not arrogant. Pick the right time and the right place.

- Highlight your work or your group's work with an eye to broader organizational benefits.

- Promote yourself in a way that is accurate.

- Don't inflate yourself at others' expense.

- Create visibility for yourself and your work. Don't expect others to notice your work without your efforts.

Consider Tonya. Being humble was her nature, and she considered it her strength. But when Tonya's boss expressed some concern that her group was not as productive as it could be, she realized that being overly humble was neither honest nor helpful. Tonya knew her group's contributions were more substantial than the boss realized. While her group's performance indicators were good, the group was not being credited for all the work they were doing. Her group often supported others in the organization, and that work was not accurately recorded or discussed. Concerned about her future and her department, Tonya took a new approach. She began to look for opportunities to talk about the group's accomplishments, rather than letting the hard work speak for itself. She added herself to the staff meeting agenda and made sure she spoke up early in the meeting. She started with a group accomplishment and a group challenge or critical issue. The information she shared was the truth; she just hadn't really shared it publicly before. After a few weeks, Tonya's boss expressed how proud he was of her for increasing her group's productivity. While the group may or may not have increased productivity, she had increased her promotion of the group and herself so that, going forward, they were accurately assessed by the organization.

Like Tonya's boss, if you manage others, you are on the receiving end of other people's efforts to self-promote. From this perspective your responsibilities are different:

- Discern fully and accurately the level of legitimate self-promotion versus the level of sucking up going on around you.

- Tap into existing talent in a way that establishes direction, alignment, and commitment in your group.

- Learn how to assess and inventory talent.

- Use and develop talent strategically to benefit the organization overall and for the long term.

As a manager you want to select, keep, and develop your best talent. But it can be a tricky business and one that takes honesty, openness, and discernment.

Consider Sandy. She is just such a manager—confident in her own skills and open to other viewpoints—but she also takes time to confirm her understanding of people's performance. Sandy doesn't just rely on what she is told by individuals but checks in with their colleagues to gain a fuller picture. She verifies performance data and asks pertinent questions to appreciate the contributions of all her employees—not just the ones who are comfortable promoting themselves. She believes that it is her responsibility to develop her staff and ensure that they are working together to achieve the corporate goals. Of course, the extra effort takes time, but Sandy considers it an important part of her role—and one that saves time, money, and resources in the long run.

So why bother to learn the truth about sucking up? Because the right use of talent is a powerful thing. When you and those around you maximize the use of your skills and your engagement in your work, you and your organization can achieve remarkable results.

Why Now?

Self-promotion is more important today than in years past. Here's why:

- Talent does not equal recognition. Many high-performing individuals and groups are overlooked.

- In times of layoffs it's dangerous to rely on the leadership to make the best decisions about people's worth to the organization. The most visible but not necessarily most valuable employees are often the ones who make the cut.

- Long gone are the days when "just doing my job" translated to success.

- Your boss can't know everything.

- Face time is limited. People are busy, organizations are dispersed, and technology has changed how we work.

- Everyone is doing more with less. People need to be in roles where they are most efficient and effective.

- Success requires many relationships. Keeping only your boss informed goes only so far. Many people need to know who you are and what you have to offer.

- Lean organizations need to employ and keep the best performers—not the best show-offs.

1

IT'S ABOUT BUILDING UP, NOT SUCKING UP

Many of the best, most talented individuals avoid self-promoting, considering it a distasteful act of selling out. They have been around too many colleagues who were obnoxious, brash self-promoters, and they steer clear of anything that might be viewed as sucking up. Often, people see self-promotion as a tactic used by less than talented people to the detriment of other dedicated people who carry the load but do so with less fanfare.

Self-promotion doesn't need to be viewed in a negative light. Interestingly, when self-promotional behaviors are done well—matching style with substance—they are usually interpreted as something else: effective communication, managing up, networking, information sharing, or relationship building.

According to CCL's research, three key reasons people's careers derail are problems with interpersonal relationships, a too-narrow focus, and failure to build a team. While some people have duly earned their negative ratings, others may have just done a terrible job of communicating about their work, skills, and talents. Effective self-promotion can be an antidote to these pitfalls.

Oops—I Forgot to Blow My Horn!

Doing a job well doesn't ensure that others will appreciate and value your work. Self-promotion is needed in some way to connect the dots between what you do and why it matters. The decision makers in the organization won't always be able to make those connections by themselves.

Consider Hannah. She was a well-respected director in a medium-size service organization. Considered to be a highly desirable boss because of her skills, attitude, and recognition of others, she led a group that brought in half of the firm's revenue. One of her colleagues, Robin, was responsible for just 10 percent of the revenue of Hannah's group.

Self-promotion connects the dots between what you do and why it matters.

The firm recently hired a new CEO, who subsequently restructured the company. Six months later, Hannah found herself in an individual contributor's role, her entire group dismantled and the revenue dispersed. Robin was put in a newly created senior executive position and given direct access to the CEO and a new, larger staff. The difference? Robin was masterful at promoting himself. He wrote long memos to the CEO that mapped out all the contributions he and his group were making to the organization. He also used his entire travel budget to be seen at client and senior leadership meetings and other high-visibility events. He kept in constant communication with a wide network of high-level colleagues to ensure that many people knew about his work. Hannah mistakenly believed that the work done under her leadership would speak for itself and that there was no need to promote it. The CEO underestimated the true value of Hannah's leadership while overestimating Robin's. As a result, Hannah and many of her former group members continue to feel overlooked and undervalued by the firm. Faced with this disappointing new reality, several have left the company; others are considering different paths in the organization. Meanwhile, the CEO is straining to recruit new top talent without even realizing the value of the leaders he lost. While Hannah inappropriately underdid self-promotion, Robin overdid it, falsely representing his work at the expense of others. Although the CEO initially gave him additional responsibility, Robin has now undermined his credibility with his colleagues. Months later, his value to the organization is severely eroded.

Ideally, the CEO would have sought out a more balanced view of the contributions and skills of his managers. And although Robin may have unfairly taken credit for the group's success, Hannah made several mistakes that contributed to her being overlooked. First, she felt that her reputation and accomplishments and the successes of her group would speak for themselves. In one way, she was right—the work did speak for itself. Everyone knew that her area was effective and efficient.

You Don't Need to Sell Your Soul

Effective self-promotion isn't about being someone you're not. In fact, your efforts will be more accurate and better received if you are genuine, substantive, and yes, imperfect. Authenticity—including an awareness of your challenges, what isn't going well, and where you need to improve—is an important skill to foster a healthy and collaborative workplace. Without it, credibility is strained and trust is hard to come by. No wonder we're wary of a coworker who is all hype and no substance.

You will be seen as authentic and credible if what you promote matches what you deliver. If you claim to be detail oriented, then you need to crunch the numbers, plan the details, and uncover the mistakes. Unmatched people skills? Put them to use resolving conflict, coaching others, and building a great group.

But what if you have the substance, but not the image or the reputation to match? Then be honest with yourself. You may need to polish up your communication skills or stretch out of your comfort zone to get the word out.

The problem was that the executive team did not know how much work she did to get it to that point. In fact, they believed that Hannah's area needed fewer resources and attention because it was operating so smoothly.

Hannah also had a hard time taking compliments and accepting credit for a job well done. She routinely deflected accolades to her group. While promoting group accomplishments is important, overdoing it minimized Hannah's own role. Her generosity toward the group made it appear that she was less responsible for the success than she actually was.

Hannah's other mistake was that she underestimated the impact of the changing political landscape. She did not think she would have to influence the interpretation of her work when the new CEO joined the company. Espousing the concept of humble leadership, Hannah knew she had a good track record, knowledge, and talent. She didn't think she needed to "sell" herself to the CEO or make a case for how her group should operate under the new structure. While Hannah assumed that her group's and her own accomplishments and contributions were known and valued, Robin went into overdrive, inflating the worth and criticality of his work and contributions.

A Better Way to Do It

Hannah and Robin were caught up in unfortunate patterns of too little self-promotion and over-the-top self-promotion. Fortunately, they aren't your only role models.

People who self-promote well understand the importance of publicizing the work done by themselves and their groups. They know that self-promotion is a way to leverage their accomplishments, strengths, and skills to influence the success of the organization. They see self-promotion as a way to build up the group and the organization, as well as a smart career move.

Sabina, a senior director at a consumer goods company, has learned how to self-promote wisely. She knows that good work alone will not speak for itself. She has been with the organization for ten years and has exemplary performance. A year ago, she took on the management of a struggling division. Sabina is very competent and works extremely hard; as a result changes have been made and, so far, the results have been outstanding.

Self-promotion is a way to build up the group and the organization, as well as a smart career move.

Sabina has gotten recognition for the turnaround. Given the high visibility of the assignment, she was going to be tied to the success or failure of the division. However, she was unwilling to let perceptions be managed by others. From the outset she let it be known that, while her approach to bringing the division into profitability was not complex or radical, the implementation would be a challenge. She shared her interpretation of the challenges with the employees in the division, as well as with her boss and the company's president. She kept each constituency updated on both successes and setbacks.

Sabina has also been careful to balance her responsibility for the turnaround with the role of others. She worked hard not just to build a group that will implement her plans; she sees that building up the talent within the division is crucial to its success. She has a competent and creative group, and she consistently recognizes group members for hard work. She gives them opportunities to present. She sees the best in people and rewards that every time she can. Every time Sabina gets kudos for her efforts, she also acknowledges the individual contributions of her group

Gender, Generation, and Culture: The Role of Identity in Self-Promotion

The way people view self-promotion is, in part, due to who they are. An organization should make an effort to recognize the good work each employee does. Personality and prior experiences play a role, as do gender, generation, and culture. While different people may prefer different types of recognition, all employees want to feel valued and respected. Each of these factors could be explored in depth in another book; however, here are some general findings:

Gender. Men and women have different perspectives on self-promotion. Women report more often than men that they struggle to gain visibility, recognition, and credibility. They generally recognize the need for self-promotion but find it more challenging than men do. Women often rely on a subtle, supportive approach to gain attention while men are more comfortable with a direct approach. Women are more inclusive than men and therefore shy away from taking credit for their own work. Women are also more likely to dilute their visibility by being overly inclusive of others when accepting acknowledgment or praise. In comparison, men struggle with establishing strong interpersonal relationships and appear to rely on their performance history and formal positions to create a positive image. More men seem to believe that the work should speak for itself and that there is no need for self-promotion.

Generation. One of the reasons employees of all generations are more likely to stay with an organization is that they receive the respect and recognition they need. In *Retiring the Generation Gap*, Jennifer Deal suggests that there is very little difference in attitude toward, use of, and capability in self-promotion between generations. Older employees report that they are more motivated by and more likely to stay with organizations that recognize their contributions—they see self-promotion as one way to make that connection. Younger employees seem to recognize the practical need to self-promote and are willing to do it to get the promotions they desire.

Culture. We know that there are cultural differences in attitudes and beliefs about self-promotion. However, self-promotion isn't an issue for U.S. managers only. On a recent visit to Singapore, for example, our Asian colleagues shared with us their view of the importance and relevance of the topic for them. They noted the need for leaders in Asia to understand the importance of self-promotion. Their cultural values often embody being humble and working hard, and they feel very uncomfortable promoting themselves. The cultural context is important to consider—that is, some techniques that may work well in one culture may not work at all in another.

There are also cultural differences in self-promoting behavior. For example, people from the West demonstrate stronger self-promotion motives and therefore more self-promoting behaviors. This is because Western cultures emphasize individual uniqueness and success, whereas Eastern cultures value harmony in the group and encourage individuals to adjust their own behaviors to fit in. However, research has found that people in all cultures have a need to enhance the self and that they promote themselves on dimensions that they consider personally important and socially appropriate (Sedikides, Gaertner, & Toguchi, 2003). Thus, Westerners usually self-promote to make themselves look more unique and independent, whereas Easterners self-promote more frequently to look agreeable and cooperative.

members. Sabina's group members know that they can trust her to do the right thing. She fights for what is right and asks for the resources she needs. A once-struggling area is now considered to be a bright spot in the company. Sabina and her group succeed partly because they have the skills to succeed, but it is also because she values her group members and their contributions and shows that publicly. It's no wonder employees are trying to transfer to her area.

Sabina's style of self-promotion is based on communication and shared effort. She is strategic and intentional in the way she creates visibility for herself and her group. Rather than using self-promotion to set herself apart from her group, she uses it to build the relationships and skills needed to accomplish business outcomes.

Leaders who are most effective in creating visibility without negative side effects do so in a pattern that is credible, consistent, and sincere. Authenticity, integrity, and honesty—along with a healthy dose of selflessness—allow you to promote your skills and accomplishments in a way that has positive results.

Authenticity, integrity, and honesty allow you to promote yourself with positive results.

2
WHY PROMOTE YOURSELF?

The visibility created by effective self-promotion has benefits for the individual. But as we've seen in the previous examples, choosing to avoid self-promotion doesn't lead to a neutral outcome. Leaving self-promotion to the most vocal or the most shameless has a cost to individuals, groups, and organizations.

If you are an experienced, successful manager, it's likely that you've benefited in some way from self-promotion. You probably have experienced the value of having a boss who is your advocate or the reward of working in a highly visible group. You may have been buffered from a self-aggrandizing coworker. It's even possible that you have gotten where you are based more on style than substance.

Even among high-performing individuals, more than one-third are undervalued by their superiors and peers. We witness this phenomenon in all of our leadership programs. As program participants receive their 360-degree feedback reports from home, typically one-third are surprised to see that their bosses, peers, and direct reports do not view them as the talented leaders they think they are. Many people attribute this to arrogance on the part of the participants, and sometimes this may be the case. However, we have discovered during in-depth discussions that the reason is often that they have not spread the word about their accomplishments. People in the organization simply do not know the extent of their contributions or the quality of their work.

Regardless of the position you've reached or the success you've had, it is wise to understand the power of self-promotion and the impact it can have. Under- or overdoing self-promotion can have a serious impact on you and those around you.

Self-Promotion Pays Off

Why should you develop effective self-promotion techniques? First, let's look at how you, as an individual in your organization, can benefit from self-promotion.

Enhance your career. Effective self-promotion often leads to career advancements, promotions, and increased pay. But these are outcomes driven by the opportunities that are created when you learn how to get noticed for your work. Long before you have a shot at a promotion or pay increase, you have the chance to take on new challenges, increase your responsibility, and work with a variety of people. These types of opportunities can be interesting and rewarding in their own right; they also help you build the skills and establish the visibility needed to enhance your career in the long term.

Stay motivated. Taking on new roles or challenges helps you build on your strengths and develop new skills. Although trying new things—including stepping out of your comfort zone to talk up your work—may feel risky, doing so will build your confidence. Imagine how great you'll feel when you accomplish something that you didn't think you could do! Plus, sooner or later, you will gain recognition and reward for your contributions and capabilities. Acknowledgment, along with increased confidence, is a great motivator. And when you are motivated, you can more readily develop and sustain a commitment to the organization and your work.

Build credibility. Self-promotion helps you build a reputation that matches your accomplishments. Consistent and appropriate self-promotion makes you a known commodity; your co-workers, your boss, and your direct reports know what to expect from you. If your reputation is in line with reality, that credibility will carry over to other departments or translate into other work.

With credibility you have the ability to motivate, to inspire, and to be worthy of others' trust.

Self-promotion helps you build a reputation that matches your accomplishments.

Gain influence. Related to credibility is the ability to influence others. Without credibility you will have a difficult time persuading, negotiating, and seeking buy-in. If you are seen as ineffectual, isolated, lacking in confidence, or limited in knowledge or expertise, you will have little influence compared with others who are viewed as effective, well connected, powerful, knowledgeable, and up-to-date. Self-promotion is a way to accurately inform others about what you bring to the table, build your reputation, and gain influence.

Not Self-Promoting Has Its Price

If you're still wondering whether self-promotion is really necessary or you still insist that only selfish attention grabbers try to get noticed, maybe you'll change your mind when you know what you are sacrificing. Refusing to self-promote does not have neutral results. You will pay the price.

No recognition = no reward. Do you want to be valued for your contributions? You need to let people know what you value about yourself, your skills, and your work. Assuming that others, including your boss, don't value your contributions can be a mistake. Your boss may simply be unaware of your merits and efforts. Developing honest, informed relationships with your boss and peers is essential for recognition and rewards, and organization-level recognition also counts. If you aren't recognized as a key contributor, you won't be on the short list for promotions, raises, or promising assignments.

Unseen = unknown. People who operate in a vacuum are not perceived to be as successful as their more visible and connected colleagues. Employees often have little or no visibility with key stakeholders or with people outside their functions. If you don't know how your work connects to others or are too selective or cryptic about informing others of your work, you won't be known for what you do and the value you bring to the organization. Bear in mind that geographically dispersed organizations make it more difficult to have face time with key people; on the other hand, effective use of technology opens up the possibilities for working and communicating with people outside your immediate sphere.

Poor info = poor decisions. Leaders are overwhelmed with work and need people who can keep them accurately informed. Without news from trusted sources, leaders waste valuable time digging for information or make uninformed decisions. Don't make it hard for others to dig up information about your work.

Promoting from a Distance

In today's global business environment more and more people are working across great distances with little opportunity to work face-to-face. People working at distances often have a difficult time accurately assessing how their work connects to others and to the organization overall. Authentic self-promotion allows everyone to take part in developing the complex picture and to learn what is important to pass along. The successful global manager knows how to stay abreast of the latest corporate decisions and keep the information pipeline flowing in all directions.

Your knowledge could very well lead to a more informed decision or simplify work for somebody else. Plus, information sharing goes both ways—if others don't see you as an information source, they are less likely to keep you in the loop. You wouldn't want to be the one basing decisions on poor or limited information.

Less visible = more vulnerable. Although competition is fierce for good talent, all employees are vulnerable to layoffs, shifting resources, and, yes, the ambition of others. Many talented individuals or their positions are eliminated simply because the people making the decisions were unaware of the contributions being made. Especially in economic tough times when layoffs are a constant threat, the suck-ups unexpectedly emerge from cubicles all over the building, much like the zombies in the movie *Night of the Living Dead.*

Losses All Around

If you are averse to promoting your valuable skills, you might just find yourself a victim of the less capable and talented. Take, for example, the unfortunate case of Tony. He is one of those people who make their jobs look easy. With the company for twelve years, he is one of the few IT managers who have unique system knowledge. As a director, he keeps the whole company's IT department running smoothly. Tony is also low key and quiet, and he would never dream of self-promoting. "I just don't brag," he explained.

When tough times hit the company and the decision was made to cut back on its workforce, Tony was let go. "I always did a good job, and I did important work," he said. "I couldn't believe I was laid off."

Luckily for Tony, his value eventually became apparent to the company. Several months after the layoffs, Tony got a call from his former boss. They were experiencing problems that no one could fix, routine issues were falling through the cracks, and the IT personnel were in a state of confusion and disorder. The manager admitted, "I just never knew how much you did to keep things running smoothly."

Tony was hired back, but what a painful way to learn a lesson! The financial loss and the weeks without work took a significant toll on Tony and his family. Meanwhile, the company went through months of lost productivity and upheaval at a time when cost savings and efficiency were essential.

As Tony's case illustrates, not only does self-promotion benefit the individual but, done right, it benefits the entire organization.

The organization deserves to have the right person in the right job. It also deserves to gain maximum benefit from the activities, information, and ideas that are generated by its talent pool. When you keep quiet about your skills and accomplishments, when you downplay your role, when you keep information to yourself—you are limiting yourself and the organization.

Not only does self-promotion benefit the individual but, done right, it benefits the entire organization.

Leaders, too, need to take responsibility. They need to be able to recognize the real top performers and those who are just really good at putting on a show. Leaders often take note of those who have the charisma or who put effort into self-promotion, while overlooking people who are truly high performers but don't do much about promoting their skills. It's easy for busy managers to pay attention to those who are conveniently in their line of sight and overlook the steady performers who don't demand the spotlight.

Sometimes even managers with good intentions believe what they're told and don't dig beneath the surface to uncover the full story. If they did, they would discover that it's usually not just one person who stars in the story, but a whole cast of characters who contribute to the plot.

More Losses

Rachel, a competent group member in product development, appreciates the benefits of self-promotion. She is the first to volunteer for work that offers visibility or the chance to look good. But she always finds a reason to be unavailable for risky, tedious, or low-profile work. Rachel's peers shoulder the burden of her selectivity, taking on greater challenges and workload. Because she is an astute self-promoter, however, she is viewed by senior executives as the star performer. She is credited with many of her group's successes and, as a result, has received praise, extra benefits, and opportunities (not to mention a top performance bonus).

On the face of it, Rachel has benefited from her brand of self-promotion, but her peers know the truth and have come to resent her. After months of putting up with Rachel's posturing, her peers are striking back by asking, "What would Rachel do?"—code for "How would Rachel get out of this work with no consequences?" Now, when management calls for people to step up to greater challenges, they don't feel bad about creatively avoiding work and responsibility.

Rachel's strategy has erased her credibility with her peers, despite her reputation with her boss and other more senior leaders. While her treatment of her peers did not have significant ramifications in the short term, Rachel and her organization are beginning to face the negative consequences of poor relationships. Her group is being marginalized by default. Rather than viewing her group as

Self-Promotion and the Tasks of Leadership

CCL's extensive research into the role of leaders has resulted in the identification of three key tasks of leadership. All three tasks reveal important aspects of the significance of self-promotion and how it can assist leaders in the accomplishment of their roles.

Establish direction. Before leaders can establish the right direction for their organizations, groups, or functional areas, they need to surface important information. Effective self-promotion can help establish direction by

- Surfacing hidden ideas, information, and performance throughout the organization and allowing a more accurate picture of where the organization is and where it needs to be

- Generating realistic and open communication and promoting a more accurate picture of the future

- Ensuring that people are working on things that are important to the organization

- Encouraging people to link their work to organizational goals

- Promoting transparency so that people will be willing to share their accomplishments and work (again ensuring that people are working on things important to the organization)

Create alignment. Most leaders feel pressure to implement the established direction, and they often fail to properly align people to contribute to the new course of action. Considering all people (and not just the show-offs) ensures realistic alignment of individual tasks, groups, and functional areas. Self-promotion contributes to alignment by

- Connecting different parts of the work by informing others

- Promoting advantageous resource allocation (getting the right people in the right places, getting resources where they're needed most, and so on)

- Encouraging collaboration

- Preventing redundancy of work

Generate commitment. Generating commitment and sustaining motivation are often the most difficult tasks of a leader. Encouraging employees and rewarding them for authentic self-promotion are essential for generating commitment. Self-promotion helps generate commitment through

- Improved employee retention

- An engaged workforce

- Motivation

- Reduced frustration and, therefore, reduced stress

an innovative resource, other departments are working around it— even outsourcing to a consulting firm in some cases.

Clearly, Rachel's self-serving behavior is wrong. But she isn't the only player in this game. Her boss has failed to see beneath the surface, and he hasn't paid attention to the workings of the group. The other group members have abdicated their authority to Rachel. Not wanting to "play politics" or "schmooze," they've decided to mock Rachel, undermine the group's work in subtle ways, and keep themselves out of the spotlight. Senior executives have also missed the boat here. Not one of them has pressed Rachel's boss to find out how well he is developing other members of the group or who, other than Rachel, might be candidates for key projects.

The Impact on Collaboration

The example of Rachel shows how sucking up can undermine an entire work group or department. One bad apple really can spoil the whole bunch. Collaboration was not fostered and relationships were sacrificed because of her overzealous, self-serving self-promotion and the leader's failure to address it. In a CCL study to determine what competencies may be indicators of perceived leadership effectiveness, results suggested that the number one indicator was dealing with problem employees. In Rachel's case, her peers would have rated the leader poorly on this because of his failure to see through Rachel's self-serving behavior and its negative effects on the group.

This example also underscores the consequences of the failure by others to engage in effective self-promotion. When individuals or groups in organizations withhold information or set up barriers either wittingly or unwittingly, organizational effectiveness suffers. Redundancies and conflicts will be hidden, and valuable information won't be shared and leveraged. Opportunities for collaboration will be missed. Competition may increase and a mentality of "every man for himself" may develop. In Rachel's case, her peers clearly chose an unproductive path. This is detrimental to organizational effectiveness; the ability to collaborate with others and to build and maintain good relationships is only increasing in importance. In fact, the definition of effective leadership has shifted in recent years to include a greater focus on relationships and collaboration because these lead to increased motivation, cross-functional communication, and innovation.

3
GET OVER YOURSELF

When we talk to people about self-promotion, the first reaction is usually negative. Some have a visceral reaction, literally recoiling at the idea. Some simply reject it; they say speaking up about their talents and successes is not their style. Others view self-promotion as a dose of tough medicine: they may know it's good for them, but it leaves a bad taste in the mouth.

In addition to holding a negative view of the truly obnoxious suck-ups, people who shy away from talking about themselves and their work usually hold other strong beliefs. In a 2008 CCL survey, conducted with over 100 successful leaders from Fortune 500 companies, we asked about the importance of self-promotion. There was a significant difference between how *important* people felt it was for success in the organization and how *effective* they rated themselves at self-promotion. The rating of importance was significantly higher than the rating of effectiveness.

If self-promotion was so important to their careers and the viability of their organizations, what was getting in their way? We found out that many people are reluctant to self-promote because they are holding on to limiting beliefs.

Beliefs That Get in the Way

It's helpful to look at the underlying beliefs you have about self-promotion, rather than just saying, "That's not my style" or "I don't believe in tooting my horn." In our experience, looking at specific beliefs allows people to reframe their thinking—which goes a long way toward making a change.

"I believe that my work should say all that needs to be said." Many, many people believe they shouldn't have to promote themselves because good work will speak for itself. In one CCL study, 66 percent of respondents gave this as their reason for not self-promoting. Unfortunately, it is not true. A lot of good work falls under the radar. Many managers are surprised to find that bosses, peers, and direct reports are not aware of their skills and contributions.

"I tend to value productivity over marketing." Another reason people commonly give is that productivity (doing the work) is more important than marketing (talking about it). The "real work" is only part of the job. Promoting yourself and your group is also part of your job and, over time, will improve your productivity. In the meantime, you just have to tell yourself that self-promotion isn't a waste of time. You can reframe it as offering yourself as a resource to the organization. It gives you a chance to share information and build relationships to get the resources, information, and support you need.

"My boss should notice." If you think it's your boss's job to know what you do and how you do it, think again. Yes, your boss has a role in this (and we'll talk about it more later on in this book). That said, your boss has many more things to worry about than whether every employee is getting recognized.

"It's a waste of time." Many people say they don't have time to promote themselves and their work. Our answer to this is twofold: First, promoting your work opens the door to greater access to the people and information needed to integrate, collaborate, and put energy where it counts. Second, investing your time in self-promotion is just as valuable as investing it in any other professional development or training.

"I am uncomfortable doing anything that might be viewed as bragging to my boss." Self-promotion is about keeping your boss informed—not about bragging or being obnoxious.

By providing information to your boss, you are, in fact, doing your job. Tell him what is going well, where the struggles are, what you need. If your boss is informed, he won't be blindsided. Plus, effective and ongoing communication builds trust, rapport, and relationships.

"I'm a team player." Your valuing your group doesn't mean individuals can't shine You need to be skilled at communicating the value of the work and the talent of the people in your group. At times, your efforts may highlight your individual role; in other cases you may promote another group member or the group as a whole. This type of promotion generates support, information sharing, cooperation, and resources, as well as rewards and recognition for a deserving group.

"I am a new leader." Effective self-promotion isn't all about you—but it is about your leadership role. While senior management does not need excruciating detail about you and your current task, they do want to know that you are engaged in your work and in the goals of the organization. Don't hang back or leave the self-promotion up to others.

"It's embarrassing. I only see the suck-ups—people who are obvious to the point of jeopardizing credibility." Nobody likes braggarts—obnoxious coworkers who think way too much of their talents. However, it doesn't require bragging to talk directly about your work, your successes, and the value of your group. You need to inform others to get buy-in and gain attention for the success of the business.

"I don't like to publicly advertise my strengths and accomplishments. I prefer that someone else do it. I would say I'm a bit on the humble side." Some people are incredibly uncomfortable speaking up about their accomplishments. This discomfort may be stronger in people with introverted or quiet personalities, those who don't have any interest in being in the spotlight, and those who were raised not to talk about themselves. If this describes you, let others help get the word out about you. Find a colleague who has a similar struggle, and make a pact to recognize and promote each other whenever you can. Just don't leave it all to chance.

"Don't make waves, fly under the radar, keep your head down." Some people believe these are the pathways of least resistance to success. Many of us have had an experience when speaking up and being noticed did not serve us well. Don't let this be your guiding lesson; it is more the exception than the rule. By all means be selective and pay attention to the politics of your organization or situation, but don't let this be your standard operating procedure.

In a CCL survey of mid-level to executive managers who attended leadership development programs or CCL Webex presentations, respondents were asked what prevented them from self-promoting. The table below shows the results of that survey.

What Keeps You from Effective Self-Promotion?

Answers	%
A. Accomplishments should speak for themselves.	66
B. Productivity trumps promoting.	26
C. Who has the time?	21
D. My boss is too busy to hear me talk about myself.	13
E. Team players don't take credit.	37
F. I don't want to brag.	42
G. I'm not interested in playing politics.	37
H. No answer	18

The Boss's View

There are many styles and techniques of self-promotion outlined later in this book that are authentic and effective. Before you decide what you do well and what you need to work on, it is good to know a bit more about your boss's perspective. Bosses do appreciate the benefits of effective self-promotion:

- *Strategic information sharing.* They need information that keeps them informed of what they need to know to accomplish their own tasks. Don't overwhelm them with all the steps it took you to get there. Play the highlight reel.

- *Consistent information.* Keep them posted on who is doing what, where the problems are, and what progress is being made.

- *Being kept informed of performance.* Bosses don't like making inaccurate judgments about people who matter.

- *Looking good to their own bosses.* Help them be in the know about their areas of responsibility and the people in it.

Bosses don't appreciate:

- *Being blindsided by not being kept informed.* Selective self-promoters who give bosses only the positive side and people who quietly wait to be asked for information risk blindsiding their bosses. Don't let your boss read about it in the newspaper before you give her the scoop.

- *Being flooded with too much information.* Everyone is busy. Don't make your boss sift through mounds of data. Effective self-promoters know how to deliver the headlines and give a good summary.

- *Competition.* Outshining your boss with over-the-top self-promotion is generally not a good idea.

- *Wasting valuable time.* Promoting for the sake of being seen does waste your boss's time. Ensure judicial self-promotion by having a meaningful and valuable message to share.

Self-Promotion Breakdown

You know self-promotion is *not* working for you when . . .

- The employee you hired last month is now your boss.

- Your colleague got a bonus for the project you have led for the past two years.

- The CEO just asked you if you were a recent hire.

- You've been working day and night on an important project, and your boss asks you, "How was your vacation?"

- Your workspace is now a shared cube instead of a corner office.

- One of your long-term colleagues just asked what you do.

- You've just been informed that you're underqualified for the job you already have.

- Your direct reports have no idea that you're their boss.

- You've just discovered the cure for cancer, and someone says, "Hey, your job looks easy."

- You've spent your life developing your expertise—only to be told that you need to attend a basic workshop in that area.

4
THE ART OF SELF-PROMOTION

Hopefully, at this point you recognize the importance of self-promotion, as well as some of the reasons that you may have resisted it up to this point. You have an idea of effective ways to self-promote and a good idea of what not to do. Now that we have you thinking about self-promotion in a bigger way, it's time to look at specific self-promotion skills and techniques.

This chapter looks at three methods of self-promotion: developing yourself, connecting with others, and creating opportunities. Of course, one action will sometimes cut across all three areas. For example, you may volunteer to work on a cross-functional team that serves as a professional stretch assignment (developing yourself). You may set a goal of reaching out to your new teammates, rather than hanging back (connecting with others). Then you could offer to take the lead in presenting team findings to senior management (creating opportunities). Other efforts will be one-time events or more straightforward, such as attending a company event or practicing your "elevator speech."

We also offer three guiding principles for effective self-promotion. These three guidelines allow you to practice self-promotion with integrity and in a way that you and others will respect and find credible.

- **Be genuine.** Don't be a fake or a liar. Take risks to learn new skills and self-promote in ways that are out of your comfort zone—but don't pretend to be someone you're not. When you build your career on an authentic sense of self, your efforts to self-promote will be genuine as well.

- **Acknowledge collective effort.** When you promote your-self, be sure to recognize the group that helped to make you successful. Speaking up about the accomplishments

---

The Worst of the Worst
(What *Not* to Do)

There's a lot of bad advice out there about how to manage up, get people to notice you, and play the game. The list below contains some advice that we have actually heard or read about and that no doubt has backfired on more than a few who have taken such advice to heart.

✘ **Always use I-statements.** It really is all about you.

✘ **Send e-mail in bulk.** Reply to all with your opinions and superfluous comments, making sure to always include the CEO!

✘ **Put on the positive spin.** Everything about your work is great! No problems!

✘ **Manage up for success**. You only have to promote up.

✘ **Spend time in common areas.** Create more visibility by hanging around the watercooler.

✘ **Become the social organizer.** Organize baby showers (while everyone else is having to work hard).

✘ **Mirror your boss.** Dress and act like your boss.

✘ **Get on your boss's schedule.** Only show up when you know your boss will be there.

✘ **Focus on the right people.** Only expend energy on those who can increase your visibility.

✘ **Do nothing!** Operate on the assumption that your work will speak for itself, and keep your nose to the grindstone.

---

of your group is one of the most comfortable ways to gain visibility, extend your network, and build relationships.

- **Recognize individual contributions (including your own).** Give praise and credit to specific individuals for good work. But don't leave yourself out. When you're the driving force or the problem solver or the effective implementer, go ahead—take the credit you deserve.

We approach the practical side of self-promotion by looking at three categories: developing yourself, connecting with others, and creating opportunities.

Developing Yourself

What are the skills and behaviors that are useful in your efforts to promote yourself? These may be technical skills or leadership capabilities that are needed to grow in your job or career and that will serve as the substance of your promotional efforts. Developing yourself also includes building skills that allow you to be effective as you toot your own horn (and increasing your comfort level along the way).

Focus on credibility. Acknowledge the positive (if you think only in terms of challenges or frustrations, you and others will fail to see the positive aspects of the work) but don't ignore trouble spots. Otherwise, your credibility will suffer. Being honest and open is important for building and maintaining credibility. Self-promotion isn't about putting out false or exaggerated information. It is about being honest, genuine, and frank about your work and your efforts.

For example:

- *An IT professional used his group's newsletter to announce his well-earned professional certifications and also how he would utilize them to benefit the group. Over time this built a reputation of not only expertise but also collaboration.*

- *During regular staff meetings, one leader allowed time to talk about both what was working and what wasn't. In this way he was seen as authentic about what was really going on and received much more help for his projects.*

Acknowledge the positive but don't ignore trouble spots.

Practice communication basics. Learn to summarize, be brief, and know your key points. People are too busy to notice all you do, much less to make important connections or understand the implications. It is part of your job to communicate and inform. Find ways to summarize, edit, and package your work. Develop an elevator speech about yourself and every key project. Think through key points so that you will be prepared and poised when given a chance to tell others about your role.

For example:

- *I have a direct report who brings me examples of completed projects that he has done. He does this very effectively—on his own without my even requesting the information. As a result he has been given additional responsibility.*

Be proactive. What are your needs and interests for the short term and long term? Let them be known! Plant the seeds for future opportunities and connections. Don't wait around for someone to hand you good opportunities to shine. If you don't ask, someone else probably will, and you'll miss out.

For example:

- *When I was traveling with our division president, he initiated a discussion on succession planning. Very tactfully he mentioned a desire to move into some higher positions that will open soon and stated why he is ready. He knows I will be a member of the selection team.*

Plan ahead. Can you answer the question, Where do you want to be in three years? If not, you need to take time to reflect and get clarity. You can then seek out the experiences, skills, and relationships you need to get there. When you have a chance to talk with a senior person in the organization, you can present yourself as goal oriented when you say something like "Leading the cross-functional team is giving me great experience. It will prepare me to take on more responsibility in the future."

For example:

- *Every New Year my friends make me choose a metaphor or word that describes how I want to feel for the year. I hate doing it because it really makes me think, but when I sit down and reflect about what I really want for myself, it guides me the whole year. Doing the same at work means you end up getting what you want instead of being frustrated with where you are.*

Know the system. It is important to understand the workings of the organization: Who are the people you need to know? What does it take to get things done? When do you need to follow the system, and when can you work around it? When you have a good understanding of organizational culture and the political elements, you can better determine how, when, and how much self-promotion is appropriate. But don't be too attached to the way things are and don't be a snob. People you've worked with in the past or people whose positions are often underappreciated can be important sources of ideas and information. And who knows? That new director may be your boss someday.

For example:

- *Okay, so you hate politics and don't like to play games. You still need to realize that if you work in an organization there is a political landscape that you are already a part of. You need to connect with people who have a good understanding of how things work. Get to know your administrators, IT staff, and HR. They have the best network across the organization, and you can learn a lot from them.*

Be an information broker. The more you release information, the more powerful it becomes. Don't hoard or hold on to it. Share the information as much as you can with as many people as makes sense. Consider your audience and find ways to meet their needs. Information is power only when it is used, not held.

For example:

- *It's not just about informing people of what you are doing; it's about moving useful information throughout the organization. Don't wait until your project is complete to announce the outcome. Instead, build in communications to stakeholders all through the process. When you hear something useful, pass it on to others who will find it helpful. Be seen as the person in the know. Information that is collected but not put on display is wasted. A person who is seen as a resource is also seen as valuable.*

The more you release information, the more powerful it becomes.

Connecting with Others

What are the strategies and tactics that help you build your network and create relationships? Connecting with others helps you to communicate in a regular and routine way with people who need to know what you do and what you know. To be effective at self-promotion, you have to communicate well with your current boss, coworkers, and teammates. But you also need to step out of your current sphere of work to make new connections and build new relationships. The following are steps you can take to do both.

Reach out. Bringing new people into your work is a practical, easy way to connect with others. It also fosters innovation and fresh ideas. Sometimes the best ideas come from unexpected sources. Invite people from other areas of the business to give a fresh perspective on a specific issue or to be an ongoing part of your team, initiative, or problem-solving process. You can draw on their information, expertise, and experience.

For example:

- *Create a peer review group. A product development group had a group of people from other departments review their concepts. It was challenging at first to hear such diverse opinions, but the product development group heard some great ideas and built up alliances they never would have had otherwise.*

Ask for help. One of the simplest and often overlooked ways of making useful connections is to ask for help. By asking for other people's assistance or expertise, you naturally have to describe your work. They may not have known of your involvement in a project, and this gives you a sincere way to talk about your work. This is a particularly good strategy to take with senior-level people. They may be too busy for ongoing commitment, but ask them for their insights, opinions, or recommendations as to who else should be involved. Once your work or project is on their radar screens, you have a good reason to keep them informed.

For example:

- *Query other staff and managers about your project as part of the project definition phase. Find out how they need to be kept informed on the project but also what help they may be able to offer. Not only does this illuminate your project, but you could also benefit from additional resources.*

Focus on solutions. You may have solved an issue that other people or groups are facing. Reach out and share your processes and solutions. If you share your accomplishments, they won't have to reinvent the solution.

For example:

- *Uncover or invent a mechanism for individuals or groups to share best practices. The emphasis should be on learning, not bragging. One way to do this is to openly discuss not only what went well but what didn't go well and what you would do differently.*

Communicate up—on your own and as a group. Look beyond your boss. Ensure that management or other senior, experienced people know about your work and special accomplishments. Seek opportunities for yourself and other group members to make presentations or attend meetings where your project may be discussed. Create a plan for who needs to know and why—and how the group will inform and educate.

For example:

- *When she described the work of people in her group, it reflected well on her, and it also showed that she cared about her people.*

- *The best examples are when leaders allow their subordinates to present their successes—combined with confident and supportive group behavior. This results in credit to the leader.*

- *The leader says, "We (rather than I) finished the project on schedule."*

Don't be shy—celebrate. When you have a big success, don't keep the news under wraps. Learning how and being willing to celebrate are parts of a leader's role. Raise awareness and pique curiosity by holding an informational marketing event, hosting a celebration, or handing out mementos. Be sure to take advantage of the company intranet or newsletter to spread the word.

For example:

- *At the successful conclusion of every big testing event, a group of engineers invited everyone who had helped to stop by their area and have refreshments. They used one wall to post pictures, data, and the final test results—effectively advertising their success but also helping others feel like part of it.*

Factor in your boss. You are on your boss's team. Be sure you understand your boss's priorities and interests, and align your efforts accordingly. You'll be in sync and you'll both benefit. It's also important to build your relationship with your boss. If you already have a good working relationship, step up your communication efforts. Learn to give him or her feedback and share your ideas. The more often you touch base, the more opportunities you'll have to talk about your own contributions.

For example:

- *When you review your performance with your boss, make sure you do your own self-appraisal. Be accurate, but not self-aggrandizing. Find out whether you and your boss have the same performance objectives. You may be putting effort into areas your boss doesn't consider important.*

Get a routine. Find a way to tell your supervisor about your efforts and successes on a regular basis. Do what works for both of you—structured or informal, written or spoken, daily or weekly. Consider how the same information could be shared more broadly. Who besides your boss could benefit from routine updates?

For example:

- *Many people are now geographically dispersed from their direct reports, bosses, and colleagues. Even if you aren't, this will work. Stop avoiding contact. The old adage of "no news is good news" just doesn't work anymore, but "out of sight, out of mind" is still prevalent! Schedule routine check-ins, and make them useful, short, and to the point.*

Educate others. Find ways to share a new skill, a new system that you have set up, or a new business idea or article. This is a great way to add depth to existing relationships—try it with your boss! Education and learning can open the door to new contacts and relationships too. Offer to train someone or hold a workshop for a group—or ask someone to do the same for you.

For example:

- *Identify what you do well and volunteer to teach it. Hold a training session, coach someone, or create a webinar on the topic.*

Create a promotional partnership. Your partner can promote your efforts and skills in ways and to people you can't or won't. You can do the same to promote his or her skills and successes. Keep each other updated about current work, but also talk about future goals and ideas for self-promotion. If your partner knows you're seeking an opportunity to work outside your area of expertise, for instance, he or she can keep an eye out for suitable options.

For example:

- *The authors of this book find it more tolerable to advocate for each other than for ourselves. One is great at writing short press releases, one has great connections, and one uses her visibility in her role to gain recognition for all.*

Make it a group effort. Talk to your group or team about the value of self-promotion. Find ways to share successes, and brainstorm ways to promote individual and group accomplishments. Set a positive tone and clear expectation so that you benefit together.

For example:

- *I have seen many cases where self-promotion was achieved through promotion of the group.*

- *A group of researchers knew they were often overlooked and decided to create a blog about the different projects they worked on. Knowing that their work was often seen as dull, they gave the blog a sense of fun and playfulness. Soon it was one of the most popular sites of the entire company, and people really learned a lot about how the work of these researchers contributed to the success of the organization.*

Creating Opportunities

What are the specific actions that lend themselves to visibility and effective self-promotion? This is the "what" and "where" of self-promotion. You can find countless opportunities to be more visible once you start thinking about small daily ways to promote yourself. Add in the strategic opportunities you'll start to create, and soon you'll have raised your profile in a legitimate, substantive way.

Accept compliments and take credit. Be sure to accept credit when credit is due. Don't settle for group credit all the time—step up and own your good work. Don't deflect or belittle good news and compliments from satisfied customers, clients, direct reports, peers, and others. In fact, pass them on. If people give you compliments, ask if they would mind taking a moment to let your boss know.

For example:

- *When someone offers a compliment on your work, say, "Thank you. I worked very hard to achieve those results. I appreciate your noticing."*

Accept credit when credit is due.

Take it when it comes. Take opportunities in routine meetings to diplomatically report on accomplishments, achievements, milestones, and successes you are genuinely proud of. Lunches, breaks, and informal gatherings are the routine activities that help you make connections on a personal level and build relationships. Be assertive and take charge when given an opportunity to lead, especially in high-profile situations.

For example:

- *When asked what you are working on, don't say, "The usual" or "Not much" or "Same old thing." Say, "We just finished an important milestone" or "We solved a challenging problem" or "I just met with a promising client." Say what's true. Don't exaggerate, but do offer a few details.*

Practice strategic visibility. While you always need to be prepared to talk about yourself and your work, you also need to be proactive. What project or skills do you need to highlight to others? What is your message, who is your audience, and how will you get the word out? A well-timed "verbal advertisement" can go a long way. You'll also want to seek opportunities to interact with senior management in situations that showcase your strengths.

For example:

- *What is your "thing"? Vidula Bal suggests always having a thing that you are identified with, or you will remain unknown even if you do good work. Whatever it is, make sure you have a term for it, like* budgeting, troubleshooting, *or* project planning, *and work it into conversations. Get yourself identified with your term by using it yourself.*

Step into the spotlight. Take on challenging work assignments or high-visibility projects. Or seek avenues for making your current projects more visible. Ask to present what you've done to specific groups that can benefit, or partner with a higher-profile person or group.

For example:

- *Take a risk. Find problems that have plagued the department for years or that others have avoided, and volunteer to tackle one of them. You might just develop new skills along the way and be recognized for being willing to take on tough challenges.*

Look outside work. Volunteer for opportunities and responsibilities that put you in a position of visibility. By signing up, you communicate a positive, confident self-image. Plus, you get good experience. Get involved with organizations related to your work: industry associations, local business groups, and so on. You can bring in fresh ideas and new relationships to bear on your work. You may even gain kudos or recognition from the association, giving you another opportunity to promote your value and expertise.

For example:

- *A young employee used his vacation to do volunteer work in a hurricane-ravaged area. When he returned to his corporate position, he took time to make short presentations of the projects he was involved in and what he learned. One of the presentations caught the eye of an executive, who created a new position for the employee that built on the skills he had learned while volunteering.*

Network wisely. You don't need to attend every employee function, and you certainly don't need to "work the room" every time. Instead, identify just one or two people you would like to meet or speak with. An easy approach is to attend corporate social events that you are genuinely interested in. For example, if your organization holds a charity event, you may enjoy the chance to give to your community. But you'll also benefit from the interaction with people outside your immediate work group.

For example:

- *There's no excuse for missing company holiday parties! Like it or not, there are some events that are must-dos. Know what they are and be there. If the CEO is in town for a meet-and-greet, polish your shoes—and your elevator speech—and be there. Show up, be seen, and be strategic.*

Prepare for performance reviews. If you've been communicating with your boss on an ongoing basis, your performance review becomes an opportunity to summarize your skills and areas for improvement. Plan and prepare so that you can use the review to highlight what matters most to you: what you have accomplished, what you would like to do next, areas for development. Just as you would prepare for a job interview with a potential boss, pull together your thoughts and information for your review.

For example:

- *Don't just review the year—plan for the next one. Have your developmental goals identified and clarify them with your boss. Check to see whether you are on the same page and ask for the support you need. Hit the highlights, outline key successes, and take credit for what you've accomplished.*

5
CREATING YOUR APPROACH

Now that we've presented a multitude of methods for effective self-promotion, you may be wondering where to start. This chapter helps you make a plan for using the self-promotion strategies that are right for you. Which approaches will work best for you given your current situation? For leaders wrestling with the idea of self-promoting, the starting point is to look at where you are, what you need to do differently, and how to create the support and opportunities that will allow self-promotion to be a valuable tool for you. You can then communicate your capabilities and successes (and those of others) in ways that are ethical and authentic.

A critical first step in identifying what approach may be best suited to you is to first determine what is currently working for you and what isn't. In all probability, you're doing some things right with regard to self-promotion and you may just need to turn up the volume. Then there are also likely to be areas that require more of an overhaul and some real changes in your thinking and actions.

Changing your attitude and behaviors related to self-promotion requires taking a good, hard look at your views of, beliefs about, and current approaches to self-promotion. Increasing your self-awareness will enable you to identify your strengths and weaknesses in this area. A close examination of your motivation and your current situation will also help you identify the steps you can take to increase your effectiveness in self-promoting.

What's Your Type?

Use the worksheet on pages 50–51 to increase your self-awareness in the area of self-promotion. After you have completed the worksheet, read on for information on how to score your responses. Stop reading here and complete the worksheet.

YES	NO	
		1. You spend a fair amount of your day informally chatting with people.
		2. You believe your work should speak for itself without elucidation or embellishment.
		3. You are annoyed when you see the same people talking about anything other than work.
		4. You spend a lot of time preparing when you know you are going to a big meeting.
		5. You have alternative routes to get in and out of your building without being seen or having to chitchat.
		6. You are a regular at the coffeemaker, watercooler, or break area.
		7. You limit non-work-related interactions with coworkers.
		8. You feel disgusted by others who reap undeserved credit.
		9. You have a close group of colleagues who know your work well.
		10. You rarely miss a corporate event.

YES	NO	
		11. You believe you should be judged by the work you deliver.
		12. You appreciate and admire others who are able to gain visibility for their honest work.
		13. You appreciate deserved praise and will offer it to your colleagues.
		14. You feel uncomfortable speaking up about your accomplishments.
		15. You attend most of the meetings you are invited to.
		16. You e-mail your project status to a select group of people.
		17. You present only the bare minimum about your project in a meeting.
		18. Your e-mail distribution includes the CEO.
		19. You avoid being around people who talk up their accomplishments.
		20. You think of your office as where the real work gets done, and you prefer to be located away from heavy traffic.

To score your worksheet, give yourself one point for every yes answer and add them up as shown below. For example, if you answered yes to number 1, give yourself one point in row A. If you answered yes to number 2, give yourself one point in row C. Continue through number 20, and total your points for each row.

A: 1, 6, 10, 15, 18 =
B: 3, 5, 7, 11, 20 =
C: 2, 8, 14, 17, 19 =
D: 4, 9, 12, 13, 16 =

Which row has the highest total? The letter of that row—A, B, C, or D—is likely to indicate your attitude toward self-promotion. When we ask people to assess their views and behaviors in regard to self-promotion, their responses fall into four general categories.

A: Schmoozer. The first category consists of people who are just naturally highly social and know everybody. They admit that they like to socialize and be seen, particularly with the right people. However, many do not see this as a form of self-promotion until they really think about it. Then it becomes clear that this propensity can be a double-edged sword. On the one hand, people may see you as a phony with little substance and a big agenda if they don't perceive your interactions as meaningful and genuine. On the other hand, such a predilection can serve you very well in the self-promotion arena if your interactions are targeted, intentional, and sincere.

B: Worker. Second are the individuals who consider themselves to be highly competent, work oriented, and productive. They view social activities, networking, and self-promoting as time wasters and a distraction from the real work. They consider such activity a sure indicator that you must have too much time on your hands and that your priorities are not the work to be done and the organization. What is critical to remember is that there is a healthy balance that one should strive for. Too much time and energy focused on self-promotion *will* detract from the task at hand. However, it is important to expand your view of the work beyond the task and take a broader, more systemic perspective. See how connections enable you to have a stronger impact in the organization and contribute to higher, not lower, workplace effectiveness.

C: Antibraggart. A third view of self-promotion is from those who see it as bragging, obnoxious, and self-serving. These individuals will go to extremes not to be perceived in such a light. They tend to be overly modest and reluctant to accept credit for successes. They are often uncomfortable with praise and deflect it or shut it down. Moreover, they are quick to take blame. Clearly, this take on self-promotion can have dire consequences in terms of the amount and kind of visibility you receive. You must ensure that your skills and your work are viewed and valued accurately by others. There is a difference between bragging and authentic self-promotion. Don't downplay your contributions.

D: Selective marketer. Finally, there are those who have a fairly healthy view of self-promotion. They appreciate its value and have had some positive experiences as a result of promoting their work, their group, or their talent. Even so, they are unsure of how to consistently and strategically market themselves in the most optimal way, without under- or overdoing it. The key here and to effective self-promotion in general is to integrate it into your routine work and communication so that it is appropriate, useful, and consistent. Self-promotion should be viewed as an ongoing leadership task—not an occasional, orchestrated activity.

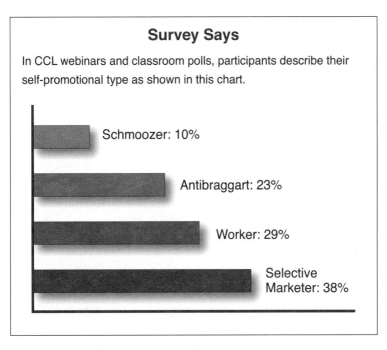

Survey Says

In CCL webinars and classroom polls, participants describe their self-promotional type as shown in this chart.

Schmoozer: 10%

Antibraggart: 23%

Worker: 29%

Selective Marketer: 38%

What's Your Motivation?

It may be that you are satisfied with your current situation and see no need to self-promote—or that you work in an organizational utopia where all are recognized and rewarded appropriately for their contributions. However, if you're reading this, that's probably not the case!

More likely, you are averse to self-promotion and have avoided it. If you have career aspirations, you need to rethink your stance. Part of this is figuring out why it's important for you to self-promote—what's your motivation? Is it that you want a promotion or raise? Do you want your group members to receive recognition for their work so they'll continue to be engaged and stick around? Identify what you want and be realistic about what you need to do to get it. Is it truly an issue of self-promotion? Is the substance there and all you need to do

Beware the Dark Side

Let's face it. Sucking up, bragging, and manipulating are workplace realities. Whether you like it or not, your boss, peers, and direct reports (even those you consider friends) may be on the dark side of self-promotion and playing only for themselves. They may be masters of sucking up. Being able to spot the not-so-innocent ways people promote themselves will help you avoid getting ambushed by a peer or coworker. Beware of the following types:

Snakes. These are the colleagues who are always poised to figuratively bite you on the heel. The key characteristic of snakes is that they do not hesitate to self-promote at others' expense. They take credit for others' work, manipulate information and people, and lack genuine substance. Be careful where you tread!

Coaches. They use their position and experience to promote themselves under the guise of helping others. They will readily publicize their efforts and not the progress of the players. Group successes are touted as their personal wins. One strategy is to offer to "talk you up" or "raise your name," suggesting that your news should be coming from them rather than directly from you. Be warned: When you play for coaches, they're only in it for themselves.

Competitors. For them, it's all about the finish line. They're focused on winning and showing up at the right time to claim the medal. Competitors will take what they can from the group or coworkers and then make a mad dash for the finish line to claim the glory. They'll come out of nowhere the minute there is an audience. Under the guise of healthy competition, they will leave colleagues in the proverbial dust to get ahead. Keep up with their pace and join in the sprint, or be prepared to be sidelined.

Buzzword kings. They invest time and energy in learning the latest jargon, read the best-selling business books, and carry around a *Harvard Business Review*. They deceive their audiences by tossing out phrases like "the global strategic talent vertical integration model" or advising them that "the take-away here is the series of actionable steps that will align our mission-critical strategies with the company's PFE." Huh? Keep a supply of barf bags on hand.

Helpless. You might wonder how playing the "Poor me, I need your help" card is an act of self-promotion. These overworked, underpaid, under-resourced geniuses act helpless to get sympathy, attention, and visibility. They create an illusion of doing so much and being so essential that no one challenges them—in fact, if they're lucky, others line up to help them out! Get out the tissues—somebody's going to end up in tears!

Femmes fatales. These flashy numbers may be male or female. Either way, they know how to use their assets to get what they want. Sexuality is used as window dressing to distract from their lack of substance. Attention, recognition, and (undeserved) credit are given generously by those caught under their spell. Beware the bling—all seduction and little substance lead to trouble.

Drama queens. They're all about the show. Highs are very high and lows are very low. A good story is taken to theatrical proportions if it will garner recognition, resources, and reward. Drama queens and the equally prevalent drama kings are fond of dramatizing how much they have accomplished, the lengths to which they went to please a customer, and the many problems they overcame to meet a deadline. You'll always know how late they worked, how many nights they spent on the road last year, or how impossible it is to hire anybody with talent—via Academy Award–winning performances. Get ready to hand over the Oscar.

Game show hosts. Who has the spotlight but doesn't know anything? Perhaps the most common type of shameless suck-up is the slick and charming game show host. These people are likeable (sort of), engaging (to a point), and important (so it seems) employees. But really, what do they do besides read the rules, ask some questions, and hand out prizes? The people behind the scenes are really running the show. Better find out what's behind door number 3 if you're playing this game.

Coattail riders. Some people just love an easy ride. Coattail riders latch on to a rising star and hang on. They'll develop symbiotic relationships with anyone who has a great reputation and high visibility. Just having their names associated with the real performer earns them undeserved visibility.

Critics. People who play the critic may not have what it takes to produce something better, but they certainly create an illusion of skill and subject-matter expertise. They'll freely criticize the work of others, but they don't offer solutions and they never roll up their sleeves to help out and get the work done. They're often eager to use your work as a platform to gain fame. Don't let these critics be your only reviewers.

Moles. Gaining special attention by providing "inside" information is the mole's method. Moles use their wit and charm to target unsuspecting colleagues and collect the scoop. Their real mission is to gain information to deliver to the boss in return for major rewards. Move over, 007; you've got competition.

is convey the information and obtain visibility for it? Examine your negative beliefs about self-promotion and don't get in your own way. Consider the following questions:

- What do you want?

- What's important to you?

- How can you reframe or reconsider the very notion of self-promotion to put it in a positive light?

- What different steps can you take?

Identify what you want and be realistic about what you need to do to get it.

What's Your Situation?

Self-promotion does not occur in a vacuum. It is a dynamic process that happens within the context of a given organizational setting, and its effects are dependent in large part on those who operate within that environment and context. Contextual factors can greatly affect what styles and approaches to self-promotion are effective in an organization and which ones derail careers. One form of self-promotion may be highly effective in one organizational culture or setting and extremely detrimental in another. It is therefore critical to be attuned to the nuances within your organization regarding the range of expected and tolerated behaviors and to consider adapting your style accordingly.

Another aspect of scanning your organizational environment is to pay attention to signals that you are not self-promoting effectively. For example, maybe you just received data from a 360-degree assessment that was a little painful. Your first instinct may be to assume that the low assessment is accurate, but perhaps it's a case of your failure to self-promote. Or maybe you have just been overlooked for a promotion that you were sure was yours. It's possible you didn't really deserve that promotion, but it's also possible that your competition pulled out all the self-aggrandizing stops. We encourage you to take stock of such situations and consider what is really going on. Consider the following questions:

- What is the situation and work context within which you operate?

- Who are the people you work with and for (boss, peers, direct reports), and what is the nature of those relationships?

- What is the organizational culture (the organization's unwritten rules, values, norms, behaviors, and practices that collectively define how work gets done and how people interact with one another)?

- What resources can you leverage?

- Who are the people you consider to be your allies?

- What obstacles might you encounter?

What's the Difference?

Where do you draw the line between self-promoting and sucking up? If honesty and substance are behind your efforts at greater visibility, then you're on the right track. Also consider whether your efforts are extreme: Do you promote only to your boss but do you do so relentlessly? Do you send an e-mail blast to the entire department describing your activities of the week? The following examples help to clarify the difference between self-promotion and sucking up.

Goal	Self-Promotion	Sucking Up
Promote the group.	Give individual recognition and group credit—both to the group members and other stakeholders.	Give credit and your attention to the most influential person in the group.
	Talk directly and honestly about your role, your ideas, your skills.	Agree with the group leader all the time.
	Give equal attention and value to all group members, regardless of position or influence.	Give lip service to the group, but make it clear that you were the mastermind.
	Present the work of the group whenever possible, both formally and informally, and encourage your group members to do the same.	Offer to be the group presenter—every time.
		Try to be on stage at every group meeting or presentation—especially when the boss is around.
	Don't shy away from the spotlight at meetings or presentations, but be willing to share the stage too.	Send out e-mail updates about your work in the group (giving the impression that you *are* the group).
	Send out e-mail updates about the group and its work.	

Goal	Self-Promotion	Sucking Up
Share a win.	Give a specific answer when someone asks, "How's it going?" Don't just say, "Great" or "Keeping busy." Know how your boss likes to hear good news—e-mail, phone call, routine reports—and send it that way. Be enthusiastic. Be able to say what you did that made a difference.	Make doing the expected and routine aspects of your job sound as if you just hit one out of the park. Overdramatize successes by making a small accomplishment sound as if you just put a man on the moon. Set off fireworks when you talk about your work. Claim that your work just solved world hunger.
Make a connection.	Ask a peer or friend to introduce you to someone who is connected to your work. Be prepared to talk about your work at company or industry events. Avoid gushing, fawning, and straining to be seen as in the know when meeting dignitaries or important people.	Only call on your contacts when you need something. Brag about your work or overstate the importance of your role at company or industry events. When meeting important people, flatter them, hang on their every word, and stay by their side.

Goal	Self-Promotion	Sucking Up
Help your boss.	Watch and learn. Figure out what you know or do that can make your boss's job easier. Do it. Step in to help your boss meet a deadline. Share information that adds value to your boss's work. Offer to take on a role or task that is currently being neglected.	Get to work early, stay late, and hang around your boss waiting for a moment when you can jump in to help. Suggest that you take on a task currently assigned to a colleague because you know you can do it better. Share confidential or personal information about a colleague or other employee if it makes you look good.
Keep others informed.	Figure out what information is needed by whom and by when. Provide it. Give periodic updates—in person, by e-mail, by department newsletter—on projects, new accounts, and good results. Be honest about mistakes, weaknesses, challenges, and outcomes.	Blast out details of your work to anyone with an e-mail address. Send out wordy updates for the sake of showing activity. Always put a positive spin on the work.

Goal	Self-Promotion	Sucking Up
Reassure.	Let your boss and other stakeholders know your plans. Communicate with details and examples to show your knowledge of the situation and expertise.	"Trust me. I know what I'm doing." "No problems. Everything is great!" Overpromise.
Highlight talent.	Recommend someone for a task or job because of his or her experience and skill. Volunteer or go after a task or job by discussing your experience, skill, and readiness. Talk openly about skills and capabilities.	Hang on to the talent in your group so that it performs well and you look good. Pass your "weaker" people off to another group. Go after a task or job by schmoozing, taking undue credit, or slamming your competition.

6
KNOWING YOUR AUDIENCE

To be effective at self-promotion, you must be well received. If your boss or superiors interpret your self-promotion as bluster or a poor attempt to gain favor, you will be seen as silly, annoying, or worse. If your peers or group members sense that you are more interested in being in the spotlight than in doing the work, you will weaken those relationships.

Different people respond positively to different behaviors. What might be appreciated by one boss may be viewed as too much information by another. We all have different talents, personalities, needs, and responsibilities that make us who we are as leaders and affect the lens through which we view others.

To increase your effectiveness at self-promotion, you need to be aware of the different recipients you may be dealing with. As a self-promoter, it will help you to understand how your messages might be received and tailor your tactics and techniques in a way that speaks to the receiver—without taking away from your own style and integrity.

Be aware of the different recipients you may be dealing with.

We've all scratched our heads and wondered how it's possible that people shamelessly sucking up aren't seen for what they are. How do such individuals continue to get away with such self-serving behavior and climb right up the corporate ladder as a result? Aren't people listening? Don't they see? Unfortunately, the answer is sometimes no. We do not all have the same level of ability, and in some instances, the motivation to accurately process such information varies. However, there are two factors that have a major impact on how people react to self-promotion—their discernment and their openness to influence.

Discernment is the capacity for distinguishing and selecting the excellent, the appropriate, the true. It is the quality of being able to grasp and comprehend what is obscure. It implies a searching mind that goes beyond the obvious or superficial.

Openness to influence, in this context, is the ability to listen to and process others' ideas, perspectives, opinions, and information. However, one definition of influence includes the concept of improper interference for personal gain. This highlights the importance of noting that openness to influence should be tempered with a high degree of discernment. Too much or too little may hinder an appropriate response.

Based on these factors, we've found that people tend to react to self-promotion in four ways. It is important to be aware of these differences and the kind of person you are dealing with so that you can tailor your message. For example, you can consider how often you should present information (and how much), how closely you should link your accomplishments with those of others and the goals of the organization, how much you need to emphasize your contributions versus those of others in the group, and so on.

The Clueless

The clueless are neither open to being influenced nor very discerning. These people do not ask questions or do their homework regarding people. They seldom have all the facts or know the whole story. The idea of going through due diligence is foreign; instead, the clueless take in information at face value. This lack of curiosity or inquisitiveness keeps them disconnected, and

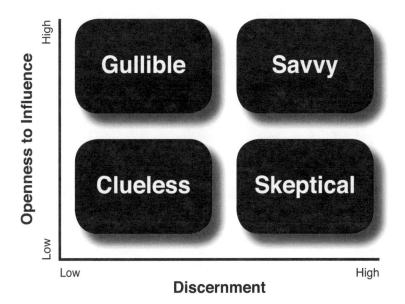

they often are not knowledgeable about areas and work outside their particular expertise.

The clueless do not distinguish between types of work, levels of success, or caliber of challenge. For example, the employee who maintains a million-dollar client relationship is not recognized any more than one who brings in new business from several small clients. An article in the *New York Times* is not differentiated from two in the local *Chronicle*.

How to self-promote to the clueless:

- Be proactive. Keep them apprised of everything you do. Don't wait for them to ask—they won't.

- Work around them without excluding or alienating them. Include their bosses in communications and communicate directly to other groups. Remember that

Beyond the Boss

As an executive coach, I worked with the entire senior executive team of a construction company. Josh was the operations manager and second in command. When I spoke with him, he revealed that he knew that Ian, the CEO, would be announcing his retirement soon. Josh knew that he would be named Ian's successor. Josh spoke to me about all his long experience, business knowledge, and accomplishments. He readily bragged that "this place couldn't run without me" and was confident of his appointment to CEO. When I pointed out that his 360-degree feedback revealed that his peers and even some of his direct reports found him lacking in interpersonal savvy and motivational skills, he dismissed the feedback as unimportant.

Later when I was alone with Ian, the CEO, he confessed that he had a real challenge on his hands with Josh. He was aware that Josh expected to be named as his replacement; in fact, Ian had encouraged that point of view. The problem? Ian and the board had selected a relatively new manager to be the next leader of the organization. When pressed, Ian confessed that he liked Josh. They played golf, spent time commiserating about divorce, and often enjoyed a laugh together. Ian was also aware that Josh had invested a lot of time and energy into promoting himself. Unlike Josh, Ian was attentive to Josh's very real performance issues and the impact they had on others. He and the board members felt that Josh was just too big of a risk to take if he did not have the support of his employees and peers.

Digging a little deeper, I heard from Josh's peers that most of them saw him as a solid performer but also a major suck-up. Because of this they had all privately gone to Ian and expressed their lack of support for his impending promotion. Josh had never before been given this feedback, and he was relying too much on his relationship with Ian to secure the promotion.

the clueless aren't usually well connected or skilled at self-promotion.

- Seek out their input and advice regularly—even if you don't need it.

- Ensure that what you do is tied to their success—and be sure to spell it out.

- Be very specific regarding the value of your contributions to the organization.

The Gullible

The gullible are typically ambitious individuals who want recognition and want to be seen as strong leaders. Because they are quite open to influence but low on discernment, they are vulnerable to manipulation by others. There can be a narcissistic quality to the gullible: most of us have a need to feel good about ourselves, but it is a strong motivator for them.

This manifests itself in different ways, but it's all about what makes the gullible feel good. Except for this Achilles' heel, they are often sharp leaders. Sometimes, they get in over their heads because of aggressively seeking and gaining promotions. Sometimes, they just have blind spots and are overly trusting of others. The gullible may not consider that people might be exaggerating or downright lying about their skills and accomplishments. They are likely to reach out for positive information so that they can feel better or more confident in what they're doing. In stressful situations they are even more vulnerable.

The gullible are open and responsive, but they are also biased about what they hear and more receptive to certain types of people. They are impressed by bling. Bling can be a person's charisma or confidence in his or her message. Bling can also be the message that the gullible want to hear, so they are susceptible to any data that supports their positions or makes them look good or feel good about themselves. If the message matches what they want to hear, they don't dig deeper for substance. If it sparkles, they want it, recognize it, and promote it. They think their stars make them look good, and they want to avoid anyone or any message that might make them look or feel bad. They are often blind to anything they don't want to see.

How to self-promote to the gullible:

- Don't wait around, hoping to be recognized. It is your job to get noticed.

- Speak their language when you can. Pay attention to the kind of data they prefer and how they like to receive information. Figure out how to refocus your message, or approach communication from another angle. How does your message fit in with what they want to hear? Can you ask for their help and feedback, to show them that you are on their side? Are there other ways to share a negative message? Can you pose a question, rather than state your answer?

- Notice what types of people they prefer. To be authentic, don't change who you are. But consider ways you can adapt in order to gain a bit more recognition. For example, if they really love video clips and flashy presentations, you might need to give up your plain black-and-white PowerPoint slides.

- Don't rebel. For example, if you know they want to hear only the positive, don't insist on pointing out the negative at every opportunity.

- Don't make them look bad in public. This is one of the worst things you can do. Unfortunately, it may be easy to do, since they are a bit sensitive about their reputations.

The Skeptical

The skeptic hears information with a very discriminating ear and is hard to influence. Skeptics process information through a complex system of filters (Why are you telling me this? What's your motivation? What's in it for you?) before they accept it and act on it. Skeptics score low on openness. They value integrity and capability, and they're highly suspicious of self-promoters.

How to self-promote to the skeptical:

- Make sure your self-promotion style is genuine and substantive.

- Deliver your message directly and without undue embellishments.

- Skeptics can smell the tiniest bit of schmoozing. Don't try it, or you'll find yourself rejected.

The Savvy

The savvy strike a solid balance between being open to the influence of others and being discerning of information. These people are usually highly competent and confident, so they have no qualms about seeking additional information or asking questions. They are also highly self-aware. They know and admit to their strengths and areas of knowledge; they also admit it when they need to rely on the talent and information of others. The savvy are not threatened by equals or those who know more, and they welcome the contributions that others make.

How to self-promote to the savvy:

- Be open, honest, direct, and not overly cynical.

- Share both sides, the full story.

- Be genuine and substantive.

- Make your case and show your value. Don't overpromote or underpromote; they are shrewd.

- Share how others contributed to the success and give credit where credit is due.

- Bottom line: Be yourself. You don't have to craft your message as much, but you still have to be proactive.

Culture of Charisma

A culture of charisma rewards people who deftly create an illusion of seductive excitement, energy, capability, and possibility. The danger of supporting and investing in this type of culture is that people get so caught up in the thrill that they fail to recognize that there is little substance behind the hype. Lone voices of reason and reality are often ignored or, worse, discredited. The cost of this dismissal results in failed projects, rejected products, demoralized employees, and lost revenue.

7
ON THE RECEIVING END

You've read about how you can use self-promotion to benefit your group, your organization, and yourself. But there is another important perspective to consider with regard to self-promotion. What if you are the boss, group leader, project leader, or division head and somebody is self-promoting to you? How do you get an accurate picture of his or her individual talent, as well as that of the group? How do you avoid falling victim to shameless suck-ups, while encouraging appropriate self-promotion that gets you valuable, accurate information about the work itself and the talent in your organization? How do you create an environment that rewards hard work, smart ideas, and real innovation—but not the suck-ups?

Leaders constantly receive messages from their peers, direct reports, and bosses regarding their value to the organization. Being able to sort through the noise and listen to authentic information is essential to identifying and motivating true talent. Listening to the wrong messages can screw up your short-term success and derail efforts to foster talent for the long term. Many of the negative consequences that result from inappropriate self-promotion can be avoided if the receiver of the information is astute in separating the facts from the bull and acting accordingly.

Selective Listening: A Tale of a Boss Deceived

Matt is a senior executive with a strong track record of success. He has been tapped to oversee a critical function of the company's product development group, which is located off-site five hours away from corporate headquarters. As the new boss, he starts off visiting the product development group regularly, but soon tapers off. He's been receiving regular communication from Gordon, a real go-getter in the product development group, by phone, by e-mail, and occasionally in person. Matt appreciates the regular updates and news of progress and activity. It appears that Gordon is making a lot of progress on a key initiative.

Matt welcomes the communication from Gordon because it's always positive and exactly what he hopes to hear. He has quickly come to see Gordon as a high per-

> **Red Flag: It's too good to be true.** You hear only positive information. You're not getting all the information you need.
> **Response:** Ask, "What's not going well?" Make sure you ask multiple sources. Encourage your employees to share the whole story—the good and the bad.

former, as he hasn't seen a comparable level of performance from the others in the group. Matt appoints Gordon to be the voice of the group by making him the formal liaison between the off-site group and corporate.

From Matt's perspective, his new efforts are in good hands with Gordon at the helm. But, as you might guess, there is more to the story.

Gordon's perspective. Gordon has been with the organization and product development group for a year. He is eager to make a name for himself. He has done a great job of identifying key players and a knowledge niche that will give him high visibility and credibility in the organization. When Matt came on board, Gordon was clear in his goals and eager to share his ideas, activities, and successes with his new boss. Because of these actions, he successfully gained visibility and was quickly enlisted by Matt to represent the product development group. In this role,

Gordon has quickly picked up on the fact that Matt responds well to constant, positive information and, therefore, that is what he communicates. He shares his own accomplishments regularly and has taken to describing the group as following his lead. He is happy to inform the group of his official role as representative to Matt and other corporate executives.

The group's perspective. The group consists of highly talented employees, some of whom have worked together for many years. They understand that one of the pitfalls of working at a remote site is limited visibility with senior management. When Gordon was hired, they saw him as collegial and competent. He seemed to pull his weight well enough. When Matt appointed Gordon to be the voice of the group, they were receptive to the idea of having a dedicated representative. They were excited to have a colleague to help influence corporate and get them the recognition they deserved. They believed Gordon had their best interests at heart.

The problem. Sitting around the lunchroom table after a site visit from Matt, the group, including Gordon, discusses the group's ongoing lack of visibility. They realize that Matt does not know the successes and talents of the individuals in the group. So the group decides to create a promotional plan to help raise their individual and collective profiles. One group member suggests sending Matt a regular update of the work, including accomplishments, challenges, and plans for overcoming obstacles. Upon hearing this, Gordon voices his opinion that this probably is not a good idea and that it might be overkill. "We don't want to overburden Matt with too much information," he says. The group pushes back and wants to find out why Gordon doesn't like the idea. One group member intuitively understands his discomfort and asks, point blank, if he is already doing this. Gordon confesses that he has been sending regular updates to Matt on his activities and successes. While the group laughs it off, they begin to see him in a different light. His credibility with senior management is going up, while his credibility with the group is going down.

The impact. Matt found it too easy to selectively listen to positive messages without questioning their validity. He continued to make the same mistake and over time built a solid reputation for rewarding employees who espoused positive messages while discounting those that were negative. Projects began to run into trouble simply because there was real reluctance to highlight any problems that might be occurring, and ultimately, Matt's group was responsible for the largest product failure the organization

---

Squeaky Wheel Gets the Grease

Jen is a graphic designer in a small company. She is often out and about, going to and from meetings. She seems to be a bit out of breath, rushing everywhere she goes. Jen usually says only a few words to people she passes in the hall, but the words are strategic. She often speaks in technical jargon and makes her work sound vital: "I am so busy! Never enough time!" "I need to get this proposal to the vice president." "We are so low on resources, and I was here all weekend working on this project." "We'll never get this work done if we don't get new equipment."

The message is clear and consistent, and it gets attention: Wow, Jen is so busy and so important—she must need the resources. She tends to work alone and doesn't delegate, so it's unclear exactly what Jen is working on. People just know that she is busy and her skills are needed to get the business. Perception is reality. Jen gets the new equipment, a raise, and an assistant.

---

experienced. He overlooked messages from solid performers that would have alerted him to early signs of problems because he preferred to pay attention to the positive promoters.

The lesson. Good leaders recognize that not all high performers are self-promoters and that not all self-promoters are high performers. To get the full picture, they have to dig a little bit, ask the right questions, and help create a culture for authentic self-promotion.

As mentioned in the previous chapter, the two factors that are key to being a shrewd evaluator of self-promoting information and behavior are openness to influence and discernment. You must be open to information about others' successes and challenges and, at the same time, be discerning about evaluating the messages you receive and the messengers.

In CCL's Developing the Strategic Leader program, one of the key competencies addressed is influence, both being the influencer and being open to influence. A strategic influencer builds relationships across the organization, focuses on the long-term success of the organization, and is open to influence from others. Being open to influence from others is perhaps the most challenging, as one does not want to appear indecisive. But if you truly want an open culture, your group needs to know that you are willing to change your mind, with the right information. To do this, you have to be discerning—to know what information to pay attention to and what to filter out. Self-promotion is a significant dynamic that plays out within this context.

What Kind of Boss Are You?

As a leader, you need to be able to weigh information and sift the facts from the fluff. So how do you measure up? Are you open to be influenced? But do you know when you're being played?

The clueless. This kind of boss is neither open to being influenced nor very discerning. You might be clueless if

- ❑ You do not ask questions or do your homework regarding people.

- ❑ You take information at face value.

- ❑ You do not differentiate between types of work or levels of success.

- ❑ You have little or no knowledge about work outside your expertise or function.

- ❑ You think no news is good news.

The impact of a clueless boss on the organization may include the following:

- Direct reports feel undervalued and unmotivated because their work is not recognized or rewarded.

- Direct reports are unfairly penalized for not performing up to par—when in fact they are, but they're not promoting themselves well.

Red Flag: You're too important to be bothered. It takes a flow chart and three weeks to get on your calendar. Have you established a complex process for employees to be able to meet with you? You are probably hearing from only the experienced and most eager self-promoters. Who else would be willing to put so much effort into getting your attention? **Response:** You need to make yourself more approachable. Create easy opportunities for people to connect with you. Be visible and accessible for all employees to share with you.

- The boss eventually loses credibility.

- The organization is truly ignorant of the talent it possesses.

Consider Luis. For many years, he has honed his technical skills and been valued as an exceptional individual contributor. Based on his track record, he was promoted to group leader. While thrilled with his recent promotion, Luis seems to prefer doing the work to managing it. He just wants to get the job done. While Luis means well, his nose-to-the-grindstone work ethic has left him completely clueless about what is going on with his group. He pays attention only to those who meet their individual metrics. He doesn't take the time to probe or connect beyond the technical details of the work. Luis is quickly alienating his direct reports because they don't feel connected to him, the mission of the group, or each other.

If you think you may be clueless (it's exceedingly difficult to come to this realization!), you need to take steps to become more open to the influence of others and, at the same time, more discerning.

- First, you must be more involved in what your direct reports and group members are doing. Be present. Communicate. Initiate conversations.

- Ask questions. Query your direct reports (without interrogating them) about their work, their progress, and their problems. Ask questions of everyone, not just a select few, and check in with key stakeholders who work with your people.

- Educate yourself outside your field. What other areas of expertise are considered valuable in the organization now, and what will be important in the future? How does your department connect to other areas of the business?

- Remember that your job as a leader is to know your people, understand their current contributions, and prepare them for future roles.

The gullible. A boss who is gullible is one who is highly open to influence, but low on discernment. Typically, a gullible boss is ambitious and wants recognition and to be seen as a strong leader. This intense desire makes the gullible susceptible to anyone or any information that makes them look good or feel good about themselves. You might be gullible if

- ❏ You don't dig deeper if you receive the message you want to hear.

- ❏ You are easily dazzled by people or projects that have "sparkle" or are high profile.

- ❏ You avoid people you consider to be downers.

- ❏ You are strongly driven by a need to feel good about yourself.

The impact of the gullible on the organization may include the following:

- Hardworking, effective employees who aren't exciting, glamorous, and arrogant don't get recognized.

- New ideas and different perspectives dwindle, since the gullible tend to hire in their own image.

- Incompetent people are rewarded and the wrong people get promoted, since the gullible are bedazzled by those who suck up to them.

- Many employees are alienated, demoralized, and frustrated by seeing the suck-ups get the rewards.

A need to look good, be liked, and be part of something successful drives most of us in some way, but for the gullible those desires are usually ratcheted up, taking on a narcissistic quality. Sometimes, however, the gullible are created in more subtle ways. Zoe, for example, was brought in to turn around a flailing marketing department. One of the criticisms of the department was its negativity. Group members were seen as having the right skills, but always falling short of expectations, bemoaning their circumstances, and focusing on why something couldn't or shouldn't be done. Zoe was thrilled with her promotion and a chance to really build a group and create some positive energy. She thought the group members just needed a coach who would encourage them and help them see the value of their success.

Red Flag: The open-door policy. If you have to announce that you have an open-door policy, you probably don't really have one. If your actions don't match your assertion, employees realize you don't really want to hear from them. They stay away from you and don't promote their work because they get the message that you don't want to be bothered.
Response: Create an open-door environment, not a policy. Make your office welcoming to visitors. Stop looking at your computer, ask specific questions, and focus on what people are saying. Consider what isn't being said (what perspective isn't being considered, what is taboo to discuss, how people edit what they say). Also, pay attention to who is stopping by and who is not. Most important, invite all points of view—not just the convenient ones.

Her main goal was to encourage a more positive approach and create a more upbeat working environment. She began to reward group members who shared good news and what was working well. She gave them time in meetings and publicly recognized

---

Nice Guy Loses—So Does the Company

Keith works at a financial company. He loves bragging about his group and their individual accomplishments. In an informal meeting with his boss, Keith brought up a project he had worked on with a peer. He talked about how great the group had done and how his peer, Mindy, had saved the day with her resourcefulness and talent.

In a follow-up meeting with the boss, Mindy referred to the project as her own. Before Keith knew what was happening, Mindy was tapped for a promotion within the group. Keith had really run the project; he was just trying not to brag. He values teamwork and was willing to share credit. Unfortunately, he deflected the spotlight away from himself and put it right on Mindy. Eager to make her mark, Mindy took that opportunity and ran with it. While it was admirable for Keith to give Mindy and the group credit, it wasn't entirely honest not to acknowledge his own part. Now, it would look like sour grapes for Keith to go to the boss and talk about his role.

Keith made the mistake of giving too much credit to another group member while unnecessarily diminishing his own importance to the group. Keith assumed that his boss would attribute at least a portion of the group success to his leadership. Instead, the boss gave the credit and reward to Mindy. Keith should have modified his approach to include highlighting his own contributions as well as giving specific credit for actions taken by group members.

them for their ideas and work. She (unconsciously?) began to cut off and discourage disagreement and negative behavior. One employee, Roni, would frequently stop by Zoe's office to talk about progress and good news. Roni frequently told Zoe what a great job she was doing and how much she enjoyed being in the group. Another employee, David, would often talk about what needed to be improved or roadblocks that were in his way. Over time, David stopped speaking up out of discouragement and, as a result, Roni got even more recognition. Zoe's own team-building vision had made her gullible.

If you think you may be gullible, you're rare. Most people would never admit their status as gullible, even to themselves. Since the gullible pride themselves on being competent and sharp, it can be a bit of a shock to think that they are being taken in. To counter the gullible tendency, you can do several things:

- Learn to separate confidence from competence. The two may or may not go together.

- Ask yourself why you are impressed with particular people. Do you like their delivery or persona (charismatic? assertive? upbeat?) or their work, ideas, and behavior?

- Don't focus on the yes-men. Learn to hear what you don't want to hear; don't get defensive or dismissive when challenged or when you hear conflicting views.

- Consciously solicit all of the information and a range of viewpoints.

The skeptical. This kind of boss is not very open to influence but is highly discerning. The skeptic hears information with a very discriminating ear. You might be a skeptic if

- ❑ You value integrity and capability above all. You are highly skeptical of self-promotion.

- ❑ You are naturally suspicious and have a difficult time taking people at face value.

- ❑ You process information through a complex system of filters (Why are you telling me this? What's your motivation? What's in it for you?) before you accept it and act on it.

The skeptic's impact on the organization is two-fold. On the plus side, when skeptics get behind someone or something, you can be confident of its value. The skeptic will readily bring up useful truths, provide reliable information, and support competent people. But this positive attribute has a negative side as well. Skeptics may overlook a person or information that does not make it through their filters. Over time, they are likely to value authentic, substantive self-promoters. However, they may not recognize or promote good people if they think they are phony or up to something. Skeptics may be seen as too negative and at times as not very approachable.

Red Flag: Personality transplants. You have direct reports who transform themselves when someone important is around—different language, different attire, attitudes and opinions that closely resemble those of the dignitary. **Response:** Mark the worst offenders as true suck-ups. The rest may be nervous or following the lead of the others. Let your group know (one-on-one, if needed) that they are losing credibility with you and others. Coach them in ways to make a positive impression without changing who they are.

Jason, an IT security manager for a government agency, let his skepticism undermine a merger of two departments. Jason was known for being very discerning with information and systems, and he had a good reputation among his employees for recognizing their work and skills. When the agency restructured, Jason's group was expanded to include another department. After six months, the group started to experience a high turnover rate and growing dissatisfaction. Senior management wondered how two groups of talented people could become less effective when they were combined. A discovery process revealed that many of the new group members felt undervalued by Jason. He was dismissing some of their accomplishments because, as new group members, they thought it important to self-promote to their new boss. But Jason did not recognize the substance; instead, he viewed these new employees as terrible suck-ups. Jason made inaccurate judgments of people because of his skeptical view of self-promoting and not being open to different styles.

If you think you are a skeptic (and you probably know who you are), you need to

- Stop making quick judgments of others. Consider the substance of the message or the outcomes of the work rather than critiquing the delivery.

- Be aware of your tendency to criticize. Suspend your assessment of others and seek out multiple perspectives.

- Don't be a selective informer. Be sure you share news and information broadly. With your tendency to categorize people, it is easy to inform some but not others.

The savvy. A savvy boss strikes an effective balance of being open to influence and discerning of information. You might be a savvy boss if

- ❏ You are highly competent in your line of work.

- ❏ You are confident without being arrogant.

- ❏ You're very self-aware. You are clear about your knowledge and skills, but also clear about what you don't know.

- ❏ You're not threatened. You aren't afraid to admit when you don't know something and are comfortable deferring to others.

- ❏ You are eager for ideas. You welcome the contributions that others make, even when they challenge your views or question you.

- ❏ You're direct and forthcoming. You expect others to be so as well; game-playing isn't your style.

Savvy bosses should be highly valued by employees and the organization. Because of who they are, they call people out, reward, and give credit where credit is due. They are not overly critical of those who do self-promote; in fact, they encourage genuine communication about people's skills and their work. This supports their ability to put the right people in the right places, helps with employee morale, and gives the organization credibility. More broadly, organizations need to have many savvy bosses to have a true culture of healthy self-promotion. A leader who supports integrity is more likely to know organizational weaknesses and strengths. The savvy can also serve as good role models and can help create key components for successful talent management.

Rosalie is a highly competent individual who has been with her organization for more than twenty years. She has earned a very positive reputation as a content expert both internally and externally in her field. She is highly respected for her competence and for her integrity. Rosalie has recently inherited George, a "problem" employee who has been labeled as an underperformer. George has been with the organization for ten years and during that time has worked for eight different bosses who, it seems, were either clueless or gullible. Under Rosalie's supervision, George has thrived. She has surfaced and highlighted George's contributions and accomplishments to their full extent. Because of her own level of confidence and ability to discern the facts, she is not threatened by any visibility her direct reports receive and in fact views it as a positive reflection on her and her entire group. Because of her recognition and support of George, he is more motivated than he has been in years, and his level of productivity is at an all-time high.

> **Red Flag: High visibility.** A direct report always does his or her work in highly visible venues— for example, the conference room enclosed by glass. Beware: This person thinks it is more important to be seen doing the work than to actually do the work. **Response:** If the work is highly visible, make sure there is substance behind it. It had better be good! Ask the spotlight hog to share the output and value of the work. Stop in and ask specific questions. If the substance or productivity isn't there, advise him or her that the appearance of important work is no substitute for the real thing.

If you think you are savvy, congratulations. Clone yourself, coach others, and keep doing what you are doing. Be aware, however, that even the savviest bosses can occasionally lose their balance. When work is really busy, chaotic, or stressful, your ability to discern may weaken. You may be too easily influenced by others. If you don't have time to dig deep, ask questions, and hear different opinions, you run the risk of becoming a gullible or clueless boss.

Strategies for Getting an Accurate Picture

Chances are that you do not want to be known as a boss who rewards the suck-ups. But even so, you might unconsciously be encouraging the very behavior that you detest.

Even if you don't fall into the extreme levels of being a boss who is clueless, skeptical, or gullible, you are susceptible to lapses in judgment. In seeking recognition for yourself or your group, you may err at times. The truth is that we all need to feel valued and appreciated. The suck-up is catering to you and may be giving you what you want, even if you don't want to admit it. In addition, in your desire for things to be going well, you may inadvertently encourage one-sided communication and focus only on good news.

As a receiver of self-promotion, then, you need effective strategies for distinguishing between self-promotion efforts that reflect substance and sincerity and those that are about posturing and preening. You'll also want to learn ways to encourage healthy, substantive self-promotion.

Distinguish between self-promotion efforts that reflect substance and sincerity and those that are about posturing and preening.

While there is no guarantee that you won't get fooled by a suck-up, these suggestions will help you minimize the damage and maximize the benefits of self-promotion.

Dig deeper. When a colleague or direct report is promoting himself, you have an opportunity and obligation to dig deeper. Due diligence is required of you as a boss. Ask questions to open the lines of communication. This will help you get more information, test for validity, and be informed. By asking deeper questions, you may determine who is truly deserving of recognition and who is just sucking up. Who has substance and who is lacking? You will also help encourage more dialogue within your group. Questions like these will help you gain an accurate picture:

- Can you tell me more?

- What's going well?

- What could be better?

- What did not work well?

- What would you do differently next time?

- How did you connect your work/project/success to the overall work of the group or organization?

- Who else is working on this with you?

- How did you make this happen?

- How did your group members and peers contribute to the work?

- Could you put together a presentation/blurb/communication about this that we can share?

- Would you be willing to present this at a higher level?

Engage. For those who need additional encouragement, engage them in the process. This will help bring in the unwilling self-promoters and can help you create an environment for open and honest communication.

- Give an employee an opportunity to shine. Ask a variety of employees ahead of time to present or share an idea.

- Encourage the expression of alternative viewpoints. After one viewpoint has been shared, make it common practice to ask for additional thoughts.

- Encourage disagreement. When done with respect, disagreement can encourage open communication and strategic thinking.

- Receiving all good news? Probe for what could be better.

- Hearing all bad news? Probe for what is going well.

- Hearing from just one person? Make sure others get a chance to speak.

Go broad. Encourage or enlist communication from a broader audience to test validity, to help promote your employees beyond your group, and to discover ways that their work is connected to key stakeholders.

- Encourage employees to talk to other departments. For example, tell a group member, "I like where you're going with this. Go talk to department B about this, and let me know what happens."

Red Flag: Your sources are limited. You have a few select people as your confidants and ears to the organization. Your informants don't have the whole picture—or worse, they have their own agendas. **Response:** However trusted those few colleagues may be, you still may be missing the big picture or the hidden meanings. You can't rely on them only and completely. You need to look at multiple layers in the organization and not be afraid to hear different perspectives.

- Offer opportunities for employees to share their information. Forums, presentations, meetings, and even daily lunches can be opportunities to introduce employees to others outside their normal spheres of work.

- Set up conversations, skip-level meetings, or skip-department meetings. Skip-level meetings give employees an opportunity to converse with someone at the level above their managers. This gives your people and your work more exposure, while drawing on additional expertise and experience. Meeting with a different department serves the same purpose.

Go long. Think about work in the long term, not just the day-to-day or even the quarter-to-quarter.

- Pay attention to the quality of performance, including efforts that are leading to future benefits even if they don't have obvious or short-term rewards.

- Work closely with your direct reports and group members so that they are able to connect the work to strategic objectives.

- Coach your direct reports on behaviors (not just technical skills) that support the strategic objectives. This will help them develop in ways that serve them—and the organization—in the long run.

Managing the Talent Show

One of the key challenges of today's organizations is talent sustainability. Talent sustainability is simply an organization's ability to continuously attract, develop, and retain people with the capabilities and commitment needed for current and future organizational success.

Creating a positive culture of authentic self-promotion for all employees is pivotal to establishing a sustainable workforce of engaged employees. Yet you probably know from experience that many workplaces are not conducive to or supportive of self-promotion, even authentic self-promotion. Frequently, people in organizations are so caught up in just getting the task done with limited resources and crushing timelines that promoting a motivating work environment goes overlooked. Or worse, organizations end up rewarding people who are suck-ups. Even more important may be an organization's ability to discern the right people to keep and the ones to let go if the economy dictates a reduction in staffing.

A positive culture of authentic self-promotion is pivotal to establishing a sustainable workforce of engaged employees.

A key feature in building a culture is reciprocity. If an organization shows that it values its employees' worth through fair and unbiased evaluation, employees are more likely to reciprocate with hard work, commitment, and innovation. In his book *The Relationship Cure*, John Gottman gives readers sound advice that translates well into the workplace. It turns out that we are all making bids toward our partners for affection, attention, or reward. Employees and employers have the same connections. The more an employer recognizes and acknowledges the bids made by their dedicated employees, the better the relationships.

Leaders can use straightforward strategies for establishing an honest and authentic culture of self-promotion. A high percentage of your workforce may be steady performers without the desire or skill to promote their good work. As a leader you simply cannot afford to overlook these solid performers. You want to make sure that the best people stay around and stay motivated.

A culture of authentic self-promotion starts with you as a leader and talent influencer. Begin by taking these actions:

Red Flag: You don't want to hear it. Sharing bad news is for negative people and for those who prefer to whine more than do. You appreciate the direct reports who share what's going right. That's how you make progress, and that's what the board wants to hear, right? **Response:** Practice monitoring your reaction to bad news. Make sure you are not defensive or dismissive when the message is not what you want to hear. Sure, we all want to hear the positive, but you could be creating a one-sided culture. Make sure you encourage and hear both what's going right and what's not.

Be a role model. Your behavior and attitudes toward self-promotion will affect the attitudes, beliefs, and behaviors of others. Therefore, you must be very deliberate and cognizant of how you deal with it. Regardless of your personal views or feelings about self-promotion, you should be willing to demonstrate how to do it in appropriate ways. Set an example for your employees. Take on the role of an effective self-promoter yourself. Don't wait for the organization to establish a norm. Demonstrate that you can be a credible, authentic high performer—and still need to promote yourself. Use your own sphere of influence and encourage those around you to practice self-promotion.

Recognize and reward appropriate self-promotion.
Create systems to recognize and reward those individuals who

self-promote in ways that are beneficial to all involved. Think about the amount of recognition you give to people and why. Make sure that people are rewarded for actual, substantive contributions and not such irrelevant factors as how much they like you, how good they make you feel, or how much you like them. Determine what their contributions are to the organization and to customers. Reward people who self-promote judiciously and substantively.

Demonstrate that you can be a credible, authentic high performer—and still need to promote yourself.

Discourage and penalize inappropriate behaviors. When you see that people are sucking up to you, call them on it! Don't let them get away with it. Ask the hard questions and deliver consequences.

Set norms and expectations for effective self-promotion. Be very explicit about your expectations. Ask people to keep you informed about their progress, work, accomplishments, and so on. Make sure people see this as the rule and not the exception. Ask for and be ready to listen to people talk about the work they have accomplished, the skills they have learned, and the challenges they face.

Coach for effective self-promotion. Self-promotion is a skill that must be learned and practiced on a regular basis. As a leader, it is your responsibility to coach those around you about the value of self-promotion, their limiting beliefs about it, and how to overcome those limitations in very practical, actionable ways.

Red Flag: You're getting too personal. Your coworkers or direct reports spend lots of time talking about your interests, your problems, or anything that is near and dear to your heart. You may be falling under the influence of people who only connect with you on a personal level. As a result, you end up misinterpreting their true level of work and contributions and ignoring the value of others. **Response**: It's appropriate to connect with people on a personal level but not to the exclusion of the work. Do not allow yourself to be swayed too far in that direction; bring the conversation back.

Realize that most of your employees don't consider it necessary to self-promote. Acknowledge this fact and work to overcome it. Be sure to recognize the work, not just the person. Highlight the many different ways people (even the shyest or most resistant) can get the word out about their work.

Recognize your own limitations or blind spots. Get feedback from your boss and trusted peers about how you are judging the skills and behaviors of people in your group. Keep an eye out for signals that you're missing key information. Know your own tendencies (skeptical, gullible, clueless, or savvy) and find ways to counteract any ill effects.

Troubleshooting: Advice for Tricky Situations

As you enter into what may feel like new and uncomfortable territory, you will likely encounter situations that feel particularly awkward. Here are several that we have encountered and our suggestions for how you might address them.

Situation: I just received 360-degree feedback, and I received some surprising data that I don't understand. I don't think it's accurate.

Advice: When people get 360-degree feedback reports, there is often a discrepancy among rater groups. Some groups rate your performance high, while others rate you as deficient. That suggests that it's not about your skills as much as how you are informing others of your skills. You may be informing some people and not others. In some cases, people self-promote up but not down or sideways. Others do a good job of informing their direct reports but not their peers. Ask yourself whether you're being selective and, if so, what you're gaining. What might you be losing? Sometimes managers see their jobs as taking care of their direct reports and buffering them from higher management. This may be a realistic view of leadership, but it costs everyone. Keeping your boss, peers, and direct reports informed and aware of your talents is essential for everyone's success. Don't discriminate.

Situation: I have been overlooked for a promotion that I know I deserved.

Advice: We have too. That's why we wrote this book! Here's what we have learned and continue to remind each other: self-promotion matters! It's a fact that many people are promoted because they are the most obvious. The boss doesn't have to dig to uncover their skills, relationships, and accomplishments. Our advice? Reread this book and use the techniques we describe! You'll be better prepared and in the spotlight when the next opportunity comes along.

Situation: An experienced peer left the company and has been replaced with someone who has less experience than I do. His aggressive competition has already surfaced, but I can't let him get the upper hand.

Advice: Okay, now you have an opportunity to practice self-promotion in a helpful way. You've already found that this new peer isn't going to automatically bow to your superior experience. You've described an added dimension of competition that our clients and coworkers report is alive and well in many organizations. To address your problem, it might help to take a long-term view. Think about strategies that are about relationship building and ways that trust and credibility can be earned on both sides. In terms of self-promotion, be sure you are being proactive and not just reactive or in a game of one-upmanship. Remember that your peer is new and trying to establish himself. You're already established, but do others really know your value? If not, find ways to let them know. Also, find ways to partner with your new peer to solve problems, rather than staking out territory. Reveal your knowledge, get to know his, and find ways to use both.

Situation: My boss is in another country, and we rarely see each other. Sometimes, I don't even know if she reads my e-mails.

Advice: You do need to communicate consistently and effectively. The key is to find out what information and performance measures your boss finds helpful. Ask. Offer suggestions. Maybe she appreciates your e-mails and receives them as a sign that you have things under control. Maybe not, but don't assume. Also, don't assume that she knows what you do. Set up a standard meeting where you can talk through projects, obstacles, and accomplishments. Avoid making the mistake of contacting your boss only when there is a problem. Finally, make more of an effort to get to know each other as individuals. Take a few minutes of time on each call to share something about yourself. Be sensitive to your audience and mindful of possible cultural differences.

Situation: I'll be going after a new job soon. In this job market, I know I have to be good *and* be able to communicate that. Help!

Advice: Interviewing for a new job is one of the most important times to practice your self-promotion skills. You can look great on paper, but if you can't follow through in person, you are likely to lose the opportunity to someone who can sell himself or herself in an interview. Prepare, prepare, prepare. Clearly identify your strengths and connect them to the job you are going after. Decide what messages you want to communicate and practice ways to succinctly get your message across. Be prepared to give details and examples. Take credit for your accomplishments and experience. This is not the time for humility. Be confident about what you can do for the company and how your unique talents will add value. Of course, don't lie and don't be arrogant.

Situation: The women in my group are supportive of each other. They always credit the group, so it's hard to know their skills and interests as individuals.

Advice: Any group of close friends or highly loyal people can have this situation. First, realize that this approach doesn't always serve either the individual or the group well. Don't dilute your strengths by always giving credit to the group for individual accomplishments. By failing to accept credit or highlight your own unique talents, you can create the perception that the entire group is mediocre. Certainly, group recognition is one effective way of promotion, but overdoing it detracts from the true strengths of the individual members. Help your group members identify what they individually bring to the table. Another benefit: with better clarity about individual strengths, the group may become more effective overall.

Situation: I'm looking to lead a project that is outside my normal scope of work. How do I promote my ability to do this when I've never actually done it?

Advice: Good for you for seeking out a new challenge! This is a great way to gain visibility. Increase your chances of getting the assignment and for ongoing success by partnering with someone who does have expertise in this area. Asking for help is often an overlooked tool of self-promotion. You'll gain valuable insight and make a good connection. Also, avoid saying that you don't have any skills in this area—because you do. You have skills that will transfer to any new project. You have to identify what they are and then make the connection for other people.

Situation: I'll be interviewing internal candidates for a new role. How can I get past the hype and get real answers?

Advice: Getting past the hype is an important part of any interview. Research shows that we hire in our own image. If candidates are clever, they will match your style to increase their chances of landing the job. One important rule is to ask for specifics and pay close attention. Candidates are often prepared to talk about outcomes (dollars saved, efficiencies gained, sales increased, and so on), but you'll get a better gauge of their substance if you ask for details about how they pulled off their successes.

Situation: I'm on the road three out of four weeks. How can I get an accurate picture of what is going on in each of my regional offices?

Advice: Set expectations and seek multiple viewpoints. Let your staff know what kind of information and updates you want routinely. For example, ask for quick updates on what is going well and what is not going well from each of your employees. Make sure you are not relying on reports from just one group member. Also, give time and attention to building relationships throughout each office. When you are on-site, use that time to get a handle on the interpersonal dynamics, elicit good feedback and information, and get to know the people.

Situation: One of my peers is incredibly talented, but he never speaks up for himself or takes credit. How can I advise him?

Advice: Share this book! He probably has a belief about self-promotion that is preventing him from tooting his own horn. He may think it's boastful or that his work will speak for itself. He also needs to connect the value of his work (his personal purpose and his organizational purpose) with the importance of self-promotion. You can help your friend by letting him know that speaking up can have an impact on the organization too. Give him an example: maybe you thought he would have been the best person to lead a process improvement team, but because he wasn't proactive, the role fell to a less qualified person. You can also offer to help by promoting his work to others.

Situation: A woman with a reputation for sucking up to the boss has just been added to our cross-functional team. How can the rest of us manage her shameless behavior?

Advice: First of all, don't go running in the opposite direction. Many times, when we work with someone who is a suck-up, we self-righteously rebel and, as a result, underpromote ourselves. It's more important than ever to give your boss an accurate picture of the work and the team. You need to be sharing all sides of the story. No, not complaining, but communicating. When your new teammate arrives, consider setting some norms or ground rules for the team to encourage honest feedback and the team behavior you want. If, after setting expectations, her behavior still becomes a problem, consider giving your colleague feedback about how she is affecting the group and the work.

Situation: I've been seen as the "golden boy" in my field of expertise, and I was just promoted to lead the group. The good news is that management bought in to my personal PR campaign. The bad news is that now I'm not so sure I believe it. Help!

Advice: First of all, ask yourself if your PR campaign was just fluff or if you have what it takes. If it's the latter, you have been given a great opportunity to shine. Step into the spotlight and help give self-promotion a good name. Now, if it's the former, you have some work to do to earn your title and some respect from your colleagues. No one likes a suck-up. Get to work and work hard. If you have the resourcefulness to create the campaign, you should be able to live up to it. Surround yourself with talented people, build strong relationships, and make sure you give credit where credit is due.

Red Flag: It's awfully quiet around here. You haven't been hearing much from your employees of late. For a while now you have been assuming that "silence is golden" and that everyone must be satisfied and the operation running smoothly. However, you just received your most recent production reports, and it appears that your group isn't operating as efficiently as you thought. **Response:** Check with a trusted colleague. Ask if you have been too harsh, too critical, or too quick to give a negative response when employees have tried to surface issues, promote new ideas, or highlight potential problems. People may have given up on making suggestions.

8
SELF-PROMOTION: THE PAST, PRESENT, AND FUTURE

As the business environment continues to change, so too must our views of what constitutes effective leadership behavior and high performance. It's arguable that working hard, being a team player, and having good rapport with the boss used to offer a decent measure of success and security. In any case, we are far removed from that situation today.

In the past, self-promotion was a source of ill will and bad feelings. No one even called it self-promotion unless it was preceded by the word *shameless*. Everyone talked about it at the watercooler, pointed fingers at the worst offenders, and got annoyed with management for its failure to recognize the consequences. Few addressed it head on or thought about their own contributions to this dysfunctional dynamic. Most chose not to play the game.

In this book, we hope we've given you a new perspective on self-promotion.

While some people will naturally be comfortable showcasing their skills and talents (real or imagined), many of us are likely to hold back. But no more! No longer can you allow a few in the organization to gain visibility and take credit to the detriment of other individuals and the organization as a whole. Today, self-promotion is a necessity. You cannot afford to sit on the sidelines and hope that your hard work and accomplishments are recognized. As tough decisions are being made around the office, the most visible stand the highest chance of survival. It is essential to the organization that the most visible also be the most talented.

As we look to the future with all its ambiguity, one thing is clear: organizations and employees need every competitive advantage they can muster. Leveraging talent appears to be at the top of the list. Whether it is a formal organizational talent management system or your own individual career path you are navigating, effective self-promotion is a smart strategy.

It is essential to the organization that the most visible also be the most talented.

To attract the best and keep the right people in the workplace, we have to recognize and utilize the real skills, abilities, and experiences that people have to offer. As an individual, you are responsible for communicating your achievements and the value you bring to the organization. As a manager, you need to seek out, recognize, and make full use of talent wherever it appears.

SUGGESTED READINGS

Bal, V. (2008, August 25). Leadership secret #1: Get a "thing." Posted to http://ccl.typepad.com/ccl_blog/2008/08/leadership-secr.html

Collins, J. (2001). *Good to great: Why some companies make the leap . . . and others don't.* New York: HarperCollins.

Criswell, C., & Martin, A. (2007). *10 trends: A study of senior executives' views on the future.* Retrieved July 15, 2009, from http://www.ccl.org/leadership/pdf/research/TenTrends.pdf

Deal, J. J. (2007). *Retiring the generation gap: How employees young and old can find common ground.* San Francisco: Jossey-Bass.

Gottman, J. M., & DeClaire, J. (2001). *The relationship cure: A five-step guide to strengthening your marriage, family, and friendships.* New York: Three Rivers Press.

Kaye, B., & Jordan-Evans, S. (2008). *Love 'em or lose 'em: Getting good people to stay.* San Francisco: Berrett-Koehler.

Martin, A. (2007). *What's next: The 2007 Changing Nature of Leadership survey.* Retrieved July 15, 2009, from https://www.ccl.org/leadership/pdf/research/WhatsNext.pdf

Scharlatt, H. (2008). *Selling your ideas to your organization.* Greensboro, NC: Center for Creative Leadership.

Sedikides, C., Gaertner, L., & Toguchi, Y. (2003). Pancultural self-enhancement. *Journal of Personality and Social Psychology, 84*(1), 60–79.

Ordering Information

To get more information, to order other CCL Press publications, or to find out about bulk-order discounts, please contact us by phone at 336-545-2810 or visit our online bookstore at www.ccl.org/publications.